7 SECRETS OF SUCCESSFUL FAMILIES

UNDERSTANDING WHAT HAPPY,
FUNCTIONAL FAMILIES HAVE IN COMMON

JIMMY EVANS

CONTENTS

THE SEVEN SECRETS OF SUCCESSFUL FAMILIES

Marriage Today™ PO Box 59888

Dallas, Texas 75229

1-800-380-6330

marriagetoday.com

XO Publishing

Unless otherwise noted, all Scripture references and quotations are taken from the New King James Version (NKJV), copyright © 1979, 1980, 1982.

Library of Congress Catalog Card Number: 2001118790

10 9 8 7 6

Printed in the United States of America

DEDICATION

I dedicate this book with great affection to my wife, Karen. For over 35 years of our relationship, Karen has been my friend, prayer partner, and example of Christ-like love. Her walk with God and commitment to me and our children have been an inspiration and source of great strength.
I extend the dedication of this book also to the wives and mothers who, like Karen, have sacrificed and prayed for their families. May the tears and prayers of the precious women of this generation and those before us result in a genuine move of God to heal and restore the families of America today and in the generations to come.

ACKNOWLEDGMENTS

I appreciate the assistance and support of so many special people in helping to make this book possible. The board of directors of MarriageToday have been a source of wisdom and encouragement to me.

I also want to express my grateful appreciation to Donna Griffin, Kimberly Fritts, and Kelli Bullard for their patience and professional help in preparing and proofing the manuscript. You always go beyond the call of duty to serve me and the Lord with excellence.

INTRODUCTION

The family is God's creation. He designed it to be a reflection of His nature, an extension of His authority, and a custodian of the culture of His Kingdom.

The family is the most essential and most noble of all human institutions. It is the cell that produces life for the social soul. When families are healthy and successful, society prospers at every level. When families are weak or torn apart, the foundations of every other human institution shake and eventually crumble. History and our culture today prove this point. Also proved is the fact that nothing can replace the family designed by God—not government, not schools, not redefined families—nothing!

From the first days of creation, Satan has attacked families with an unholy vengeance. He persists today, knowing that if he wages a successful campaign against the family, he can sabotage God's purposes and keep them from being accomplished in our lives. Satan views hurting, dysfunctional families as trophies in his war against God. The more he collects, the more he celebrates certain victory. Surely, as he scans the social horizon of America today, he is congratulating himself and his evil underlings for the severe damage they have inflicted upon the family.

Satan isn't the only one who understands the strategic importance of family. God has instituted a plan that depends upon the wholeness and proper functioning of marriages and families. Therefore, with all the authority of heaven and earth, He fights for the family. In America today, God delivers a standard of truth to those who are ignorant, a message of forgiveness for those who have failed, and a heart of compassion for those who have been wounded in the fight. God, not Satan, will win this war; and in the end, the family will be redeemed to accomplish God's original purpose.

I have written this book with the belief that God has led me to do so. I pray that it will be helpful to those who are seeking God's will for their families. Regardless of whether you have a good family and are desiring greater satisfaction, or you are coming from a failed and dysfunctional environment, I believe the contents of this book will help you.

The following chapters explain seven essential traits of a happy, successful family. I truly believe these key areas represent Biblical, universal truths that properly reflect God's design for every family, regardless of those factors that distinguish individuals. As you read, I hope you will observe and be encouraged by the fact that even though failure and dysfunction are common among families today, they are preventable and reversible. Family success has nothing to do with luck or fate and has everything to do with obedience and submission to God and His eternal truths. Therefore, any person who is willing to follow God's pattern for family life will succeed. That's good news!

Regardless of who we are, how badly we've failed, how deeply we've been hurt, or the condition of our lives today, God has the power to heal us, transform us, and guide us to paths of life. I pray that the contents of this book will be used by God to further these purposes in your life and family.

—*Jimmy Evans*

SECRET ONE

A Correct Priority Structure

*But seek first the kingdom of God and His righteousness, and all
these things shall be added to you.*
Matthew 6:33

---

*"Teacher, which is the great commandment in the law?" Jesus said
to him, "'You shall love the Lord your God with all your heart,
with all
your soul, and with all your mind.' This is the first and great
commandment. And the second is like it: 'You shall love your
neighbor as yourself.'"*
Matthew 22:36–39

The Bible is crystal clear regarding our priorities. We are
commanded by God to put Him first and people second. In fact,
Matthew 6:33 conveys a powerful promise for the person who puts
God first: "*... all these things shall be added to you.*" "All these things"

refers to the comforts, wealth, position in life, and security we are seeking. The context of the promise began as Jesus was chastising His disciples for their unbelief toward God and their anxiety concerning life's provision. He finalized His discourse by promising faithful and complete blessings for the person who gives God priority above all else.

The establishing of priorities in our lives and families is a high-stakes issue. It means the difference between being blessed or battered, intimate or enemies, a success or a statistic. Successful families are always families with a correct priority structure purposefully entrenched in their lives. It doesn't happen by accident. It happens because they make the choice to arrange their decisions, practices, and lifestyles to honor God first and then family.

Even though most Christians agree that God should be first and family should come next, much of our agreement is simply lip service that doesn't translate into our everyday lives. We must understand that the *intention* to have correct priorities doesn't benefit us or our families. An old adage even suggests that, "the road to ruin is paved with good intentions" (my paraphrase). Until good intent unites with the willingness to make the difficult daily choices and to say no to competing demands, we won't find the blessing and harmony for which we are looking.

Three important truths concerning priorities

There are three important truths, which can help you understand the importance of Biblical priorities and encourage you to pay whatever price is necessary to establish them in your life.

1. Priorities demonstrate our value system as well as the value system we will pass on to our children.

Our priorities *are* our values. The person who gives priority to God values God. The person who gives something priority above God values something more than God. It is that simple. The same is true of family; the person who gives priority to family highly values family.

The essence of hypocrisy is speaking something that we are unwilling to live. The truth is, many of us are simply hypocritical concerning our priorities. Much of the disappointment and disharmony in our personal lives and families is a fruit of our sin. For instance, a man may say he loves his wife, but chooses work or sports above her. Parents say they love their children, but allow them to be crowded out of their daily schedules by something that is less important. We say we love God first, but are unwilling to sacrifice in order to give, worship, or serve Him. This is hypocrisy.

When God examines our priorities, His scrutiny isn't placed primarily on what we say we believe; it is on what we practice. When God sees us putting Him first, He knows we value Him; therefore, He blesses us. However, when He sees that something has replaced Him in our lives—not that we have renounced Him or changed our minds about Him, but that we have simply reprioritized Him to a position less than first—He knows He is being devalued. Also, He views as an idol whatever has taken His place, even if it is something good and necessary. Even though God always loves us, He simply will not bless a life that has devalued Him and is practicing idolatry.

Not only is there a breakdown of relationship between God and us when our priorities are wrong, but also the same thing is true of our relationships with our spouses. God's first commandment related to marriage in Genesis 2:24 is that we must "leave" our fathers and mothers. The word "leave" doesn't mean that we forsake or neglect our parents in favor of our spouses; it simply means that our marriage has priority above them.

In fact, not only must we give our marriage priority above our parents, we must do the same in every area in life, with the exception of God. When we do this, it creates an environment of energy and affection for our marriage. When we don't, jealousy and hurt feelings occur. Our spouses intuitively know that they should have priority above everything other than God. The importance of this issue in marital satisfaction cannot be overstated or underestimated.

Our children will also reflect whether they feel they have a position of priority. Even though all children have their problems, children who feel unloved and rejected by their parents have much greater problems and cause much more heartache. Parenting is a full-time job that requires a great deal of time and energy.

Except for God and our spouses, nothing should be valued greater than our children. Regardless of what else we must sacrifice, we must not sacrifice the time, attention, energy, and love we devote to our kids. They need to know in real terms that they are precious and important to us.

In addition to gaining the blessing of God and our families, we also transmit correct values to our children when our priorities are right. We must realize that our children's future happiness and success aren't primarily dependent on education, relationships, or income.

They are based on whether or not God is blessing them. God's approval brings peace and prosperity to us without grief, stress, or relational difficulties.

> *"The blessing of the LORD makes one rich, and He adds no sorrow with it"*
> Proverbs 10:22

Therefore, as parents, we must train our children through godly example to honor Biblical priorities. As we do, both we and they are ensured of God's blessings.

2. Right priorities promote the health and growth of the most important things in our lives. Wrong priorities prohibit growth and health.

When Karen and I married, I was obsessed with golf and work. Those two things consumed my primary energy, both physically and emotionally. At the end of my pursuits at work or at a game of golf, I had little time or energy left for Karen, for our children, or for God.

The result was a family life that was miserable and filled with tension.

Even though I insisted that I loved God, Karen, and my children before all else, I was distant and grew more emotionally separated from each of them. When confronted by Karen about my failure as a man of God, husband, and father, I became angry. My greatest indignation was over her labeling me a hypocrite. She told me that I kept saying things I didn't really mean. When she said that (and she said it often), I would retaliate with a self-congratulating sermon, reminding her how wonderful I was and how much I did for her and the kids. Even though my little speeches sometimes got her off my back, the tension remained.

Our marriage finally came to a breaking point. The central issue was whether or not I would give priority to God and my family above my work and the time I spent playing golf. Even though it was over thirty years ago, I remember the moment I made that decision. It was gut wrenching. I thought I had lost everything and become a domestic martyr. I was ignorant.

I look back on that event now as being one of the greatest turning points in my life. Today, not only do I have a great career and still enjoy golf, but I also have a fulfilling, growing, intimate relationship with God, Karen, and my children. Truly, I have it all. Why? Because I finally got my priorities straight.

Biblical priorities are protective parameters that keep the most important things as the most important things. Priorities are made evident by how we spend our time, energy, and money. If we give the first of these things to God, God stays first in our lives, and our relationship with Him flourishes. When we don't give the best to Him, our relationship suffers and stops growing. There is never an exception to this truth.

A powerful example of this point is found in a verse of Scripture in Matthew 6:21. Jesus said,

"For where your treasure is, there your heart will be also."

The Greek word for "treasure" used in this verse is the word *thesauros*. It means "a treasure or treasury." The word "heart" is the Greek word *kardia*, which means "our inner self or the seat of our emotions." The significance of these words in this verse is powerful. What Jesus is telling us is that our real feelings and focus will be wherever we establish the place(s) to deposit and secure what we treasure (time, energy, money).

It is impossible to separate your treasure and your heart. It can't be done. For example, if your treasury is your job—if that's the place you give the best and/or most of your treasures—then your feelings and focus will be there. If your treasury is school, your heart will be at school. If your treasury is a sport or hobby, then your feelings and focus will be there. If your treasury is in God and your family, your primary passions and desires will be there.

Beyond the truth of this principle, there is another aspect of it that has powerful implications. It has to do with changing our feelings toward something or someone. An example is my relationship with God and my family early in my marriage. I had a strong mental and emotional connection to my job and to golf, but my desires for God and my family were minimal.

Today, everything has changed. I feel more desire and passion toward God, Karen, and my children than I have ever felt; and the desire and passion keep growing. How did things change? It wasn't because I had a magical, emotional experience that caused me to wake up one morning in love with all the right people. It is because I made a decision of my will, which was contrary to my emotions, that I was going to change the place where I was investing the primary treasures of my life.

When I made a deliberate effort to give the best of my treasures to God and my family, my emotions followed. To my surprise, I fell deeply in love with God and my family. It is an eternal truth I have experienced personally.

Regardless of what your emotions are telling you today, honestly examine where you are giving your best. If it is not with God and your family, you are making a mistake. That mistake will not only prohibit growth in your relationships, but it will also create serious problems and emotional pain. If you realize you are investing in the wrong place, repent before God and your family and change. No matter what you must give up, you will find that the rewards far outweigh the cost— regardless of how high it might seem to you today. I am living proof.

America is a culture that wants it all. The irony is that we have gained everything material and external and lost everything meaningful in the process. Our culture has laid God and family on the altar of our pleasure and success, only to find that what we have gained is empty when we don't have peace within our hearts and homes. Today, many people are waking to the truth that things don't bring happiness; peace with God and family brings happiness and fulfillment—even in the absence of everything else.

3. The three essential priorities are God, family, and church.

I realize there are some priorities that we may not have in common. Just because we don't totally conform with other people doesn't mean we're wrong; it just means we're different, and that's fine. However, there are three priorities that are essential, universal, and unchanging: God, family, and church.

Some people are surprised at the separation between God and church. Many believe that devotion to church is equal to devotion with God. Even though there is an obvious connection, there is also a very important distinction, and both are essential.

Our devotion to God is a personal issue. It has to do with personal prayer, obedience to God's Word, and giving God the first and best of our lives every day in every arena of life. Is it possible to be highly involved in church without really giving priority to God in our lives? Yes, it is. In fact, it is sadly common. The Pharisees with whom Jesus dealt are perfect examples. They were masters of religion who had hollow hearts. Even though they cherished their traditional exercises of religion and practiced them with zeal, they didn't place God first.

We need to be careful not to confuse God and church. Giving God priority means that we seek and serve Him on a personal level moment by moment. It means that He goes where we go and that He is invited as Lord into our relationships, financial decisions, traumas, successes, conversations, and thought lives. This issue is much broader than our commitment to church.

After making that point, let me now emphasize the importance of church. For people who have made a commitment to God and family, it is essential to have a support network of like-minded people. The church is not only an institution ordained by God to spread the Gospel, but it is also a relational base of accountability, spiritual support, and encouragement for the saints.

The church has made a dramatic impact on my life, marriage, and family. When Karen and I had problems early in our marriage, it was our Sunday school teachers who took us out to eat, offered us godly counsel, and encouraged us through their own experiences. Our participation with other young couples from church who were committed to God and their marriages inspired us and kept us from going the way of many of our friends who were divorcing and having affairs.

When we became parents, the church grew to be an important extension of us to our children. Church and Sunday school reinforced in our kids what we were teaching at home. The children's and youth groups at the church became places where our children were discipled in God's Word, and where they built important relationships, which they still have today. I shudder at the thought of what would have become of us and our children had it not been for our precious group of church friends.

As I have counseled couples through the years, I have found a common thread in those who don't succeed. Most often they are surrounded by negative companions and bad examples. The Bible has something to say about this. First Corinthians 15:33 says,

"Do not be deceived: 'Evil company corrupts good habits.'"

One of the best places to develop healthy, godly relationships is at church. But some people think they are the exception —too cool for God. So they disregard this option while they continue to keep or build their primary relationships with non-Christians or non-practicing Christians.

Not only do these people lack the weekly accountability and spiritual support from fellow believers, but they are also constantly exposed to wrong examples, wrong thinking, and wrong advice. In that environment, even the strongest Christian in the world will be worn down in time. Therefore, just as I Corinthians 15:33 says that good habits won't redeem the bad company around you when you're separated from regular church fellowship, so, too, will bad company corrupt and rob you of precious spiritual treasures. This same truth also applies in a very profound way to children. They are highly affected by their peer group. Accordingly, direct parental oversight related to their friends and overall circumstances is essential.

As we establish daily disciplines in our lives (prayer, Bible reading, quality time for our spouses and children, and so on), we must also establish regular weekly times for church. First of all, look for a good, loving, Bible-believing church. Don't attend a legalistic church or a liberal one. Find a church where they believe in the authority of Scripture with an attitude of grace.

Even though there is no perfect church, God will faithfully lead us to the church that is best for us when we prayerfully seek His will. Once we commit ourselves to a local church, we need to attend the weekly worship services faithfully, become a part of a weekly Bible study or small sharing and prayer group, and find a place to serve. We need to make sure our children are a part of weekly worship with us (especially as they get older) and a part of a Sunday school class for their age. These disciplines for our children and us are very important.

Biblical priorities are an essential part of a healthy family life. Establishing them may be uncomfortable or just downright hard. However, the benefits are awesome; the longer you live with correct priorities, the more blessings you will see, and the easier and more natural a rightly prioritized life becomes.

One more point related to priorities. After you've established them, you must then protect them. Even though we don't need to be legalistic, we do need to be firm in our commitment to keep our priorities right. This means we may have to put a lot of time into our work for a short season, but we don't let it continue for long.

It means that we may miss church for a week or two because of vacation or sickness, but we don't allow ourselves to get into the habit of missing. Priorities aren't an exact science all of the time, but they are an eternal principle all of the time. God doesn't demand legalistic conformity, but He does require honest commitment to do what we know is right and to repent and change when we are wrong.

Begin to look around you. You'll notice something. Successful families have practices, habits, and traditions that keep them on course. They may look easy from the outside, but they require effort. It is this conscious, consistent work that makes a successful family. Daily pains to live correctly bring God's blessings and produce noticeable gains for a marriage and family. A successful family is no accident. It begins with a commitment to establish and maintain right priorities.

With daily dependence upon God and a solid commitment to never give up or surrender, we can make it. I started more than thirty years ago on my journey. I was ignorant and immature, but I made up my mind that I would pay whatever price was necessary to get things right with God and my family. Even though my commitment was essential, God was so gracious to help me and to pick me up when I failed. Today, I'm happy, and I'm different. The same God who helped me will help you! If you haven't already done so, make a commitment now to God and your family. Put them and keep them where they belong. A life of blessing will follow.

The law of the Lord is perfect, converting the soul;
The testimony of the Lord is sure, making wise the simple; The
statutes of the Lord are right, rejoicing the heart;
The commandment of the Lord is pure, enlightening the eyes; The
fear of the Lord is clean, enduring forever;

The judgments of the Lord are true and righteous altogether.
More to be desired are they than gold, Yea, than much fine gold;
Sweeter also than honey and the honeycomb. Moreover by them
Your servant is warned, And in keeping them there is great reward.

Psalm 19:7–11

SECRET TWO

A Balance of Grace and Truth

*And the Word became flesh and dwelt among us, and we beheld His glory, the glory as of the only begotten of the Father, **full of grace and truth**.*
John 1:14 (emphasis added)

Jesus Christ was more than a sinless man; He was a flawless illustration of the nature of God. In perfect balance, the life of Jesus simultaneously revealed the glory of God and the pattern of a perfect human life. As God, Jesus was the clear and unwavering expression of eternal truth— thus He is called "the Word." As man, Jesus revealed how "flesh" could live according to God's standards through a yielded, Spirit-led life.

Even though the life of Christ was a stark contrast of humanity and divinity, a common thread of character flowed through each side. The Apostle John used his unique insights into the nature of Christ to reveal the essence of the common character traits of Jesus that filled and fueled Him as both the Son of God and Son of man. According to John 1:14, the two primary forces that motivated Christ were "grace and truth." John says He was "full" of these things. The word used for "full" in John 1:14 means that every area of Jesus' being was totally permeated with these two elements.

John's revelation of Jesus is invaluable in understanding the nature of God and the secret of successful family relationships. Just as Jesus was a perfect balance of grace and truth, every successful relationship must be balanced with these two elements. In every relationship, truth is the essential ingredient that bears a standard and prevents violation or moral degeneration. However, truth by itself is cruel, intimidating, and counterproductive.

Grace is the essential relational ingredient that values and elevates. Grace isn't focused on performance, but on the desire to be united in heart with the object of its affection. Grace is the ointment that makes truth bearable, the sweet fragrance that beautifies an imperfect garden. Grace never argues or disagrees with God's standards, but accepts, forgives, and encourages the one who is struggling to attain to truth.

Grace and truth are inseparable partners. Truth by itself kills. It is a harsh taskmaster with no loyal subjects. Grace by itself is a cheerleader without a team—a spineless organism without strength or definition.

Consider these tenets:

Relationships of truth without grace dry up Relationships of grace without truth blow up Relationships of truth *and* grace grow up

These are universal, eternal truths that are based upon God's nature and the way He created us to function.

A powerful example of the critical need for a balance of grace and truth in all relationships is found in the Old Testament story of the Ark of the Covenant. God commanded Moses in Exodus 25 to build two pieces of furniture that when united together would be a physical representation of God to Israel.

The first of the two pieces was an ark. The ark was a trunk-like receptacle that Moses was instructed to fill with the tablets of stone containing the Ten Commandments, his brother Aaron's rod that budded, and a pot of manna. The ark and its contents symbolized the perfection of God and the eternal standards of His character.

The Ten Commandments represented God's perfect law. The rod of Aaron represented God's perfect authority. The pot of manna represented God's perfect faithfulness to mankind. Therefore, when completed, the ark and its contents were a powerful representation of the unchangeable standards of God's perfection.

Even though it was significant by any standard, the ark by itself was incomplete. Another piece of furniture was built to cover the ark and its priceless contents. Unlike the plain, rectangular ark below, the piece of furniture built to cover the ark was magnificent.

It was called the "mercy seat." Covered in pure gold, the mercy seat was surrounded by two golden cherubim (angels) with their wings outstretched. Once a year, an unblemished lamb was sacrificed, and its blood was poured on the mercy seat for the forgiveness of sins for the tribes of Israel. This, of course, was Old Testament symbolism for the coming sacrifice of Christ, of whom John the Baptist would later say,

> *"Behold! The Lamb of God who takes away the*
> *sin of the world!"*
> John 1:29

The ark and the mercy seat united together were called the "Ark of the Covenant." God was communicating to Israel through the ark about His nature and the way He related to man. The point was this: God is full of grace and truth. These two indivisible elements permeate His being and represent His divine character.

Once the ark was completed, God commanded Moses to put it behind a tent curtain in the Tabernacle. This enclosure was called the "Holy of Holies." Only one man, the High Priest, once a year, could see the glory of the ark. However, when Jesus died on the cross, the Bible tells us that the curtain of the Holy of Holies was ripped from top to bottom (Matthew 27:51) and the Holy of Holies was transferred from Mount Zion in Jerusalem to the human heart. We are now the temple of the Spirit of God (I Corinthians 6:19), and our hearts are the Holy of Holies. The divine presence that once filled two united pieces of furniture now wants to fill us.

This is such an important issue to understand. God created us in His image (Genesis 1:27). What is His image? There are many dimensions to this issue, but as it relates to God's character, His image is "grace and truth." The person who is full of grace and truth is Christlike.

A person without grace isn't Christlike, nor is a person who rejects truth. It is the combined operation of grace and truth in our marriages, families, and other relationships that reflects God's divine imprint. Only when both elements are present and balanced can we attain to the blessing and order of God that produces healthy, successful relationships.

Returning to the story of the ark, an example of the extreme danger of separating grace and truth was illustrated powerfully in I Samuel 6:19. The Philistines, archenemies of Israel, had gained possession of the ark, but to their peril. While a blessing to the children of Israel, the ark was a curse in the hands of the Philistines. As long as they had the ark, they experienced plagues and tumors and all kinds of anguish. Thus, they returned the ark to Israel.

Jubilant over the return of the ark, the men of Beth Shemesh watched as the gleaming angels' wings drew closer on an ox-drawn cart. Shouting from house to house and village to village, they raced toward the ark, which symbolized God's presence and blessing. As thousands of them gathered around the ark in celebration, someone made a fatal mistake. Without understanding the critical connection between the ark below and the mercy seat above, they separated the two pieces of furniture.

Lifting the golden mercy seat away with the hopes of seeing the tablets of stone with the engraved commandments and the other articles they had heard about all of their lives, the men of Beth Shemesh thought they were on the verge of experiencing a glorious dream. Instead, they experienced their worst nightmare. According to

I Samuel 6, when they separated the ark from the mercy seat, 50,070 men died immediately. The shock from the disconnected ark shattered Israel that day. Shaking their heads in grief and disbelief, the people of Israel wondered if the presence of God through the ark was a blessing or a curse.

Of course, God's presence is a blessing. However, just as in the days of the ark in Israel, many people today have been raised in homes and/or churches that present an imbalanced view of God. They have cracked the lid on the ark, and destruction has resulted. An example is a man I counseled for years who was raised in a "hellfire-and-brimstone" preaching church.

Every day of his childhood was lived in insecurity and the fear of eternal punishment. His parents and pastor constantly told him that he fell below God's standards and that the only security he could have was to live a "holy" life. Thus, as an adult, he lived in constant insecurity, a driving force for him and his family.

One of the most powerful determining factors of our concept of God is the character of our parents and the relational atmosphere of the home in which we were raised.

One of the most powerful determining factors of our concept of God is the character of our parents and the relational atmosphere of the home in which we were raised. Even though a "free" life looks beautiful from a distance, when removed from truth, it is deadly.

At the very root of how our families function, there is a deeper foundation that we need to examine as it relates to balance. In order for us to be relationally healthy, we need to examine our concept of God to make sure it is correct. One of the most powerful determining factors of our concept of God is the character of our parents and the relational atmosphere of the home in which we were raised. Instinctively, we relate to God based on our parents and how they related to us. Therefore, if our parents were imbalanced toward grace or truth, it is common for us to view God in the same way.

Regardless of how any of us were raised, God isn't defined by our past; He is defined by who the Word of God says He is, a God permeated with an inseparable balance of grace and truth. He is a

God of unwavering standards motivated by a heart of compassion and mercy. He won't give up grace for truth or truth for grace. You get the whole package, or you get a false god.

Once we understand the importance of this balance in God and our concept of Him, we then need to examine our own personalities to see if we are balanced. As spouses or parents, we must realize that our ability to have healthy relationships is based on a balance of grace and truth. However, most of us have a natural imbalance we need to acknowledge and overcome.

An example of how our personalities are naturally imbalanced can be found in four basic temperament traits observed for centuries. These are commonly called choleric, melancholy, sanguine, and phlegmatic. For our purposes, we will call these the lion, beaver, otter, and golden retriever temperaments. These are labels I've borrowed from Gary Smalley, who does an excellent job of helping us understand our temperaments, especially regarding marriage and family relationships.

Here is a brief definition and explanation of each of the four temperaments:

- **Lion** (choleric)—confident, decisive, opinionated. *Makes a good leader.*
- **Beaver** (melancholy)—organized, methodical, systematic. *Makes a good administrator.*
- **Otter** (sanguine)—fun, personable, spontaneous. *Makes a good salesperson or public relations representative.*
- **Golden Retriever** (phlegmatic)—stable, consistent, loyal. *Makes a good friend and/or trusted employee.*

All of us have a combination of these temperament traits that make up our personalities. However, one temperament usually dominates in most of us. For example, I know I am primarily a lion temperament, and my wife, Karen, is a golden retriever—but we both have some melancholy also.

As it relates to a balance of personality, we need to realize that every temperament trait has a natural imbalance. Both the lion and beaver temperaments are imbalanced toward truth. The lion temperament has a tendency to prioritize issues and progress over people. It isn't uncommon for a lion to be very difficult to live with because he or she can be bossy and dominating. Without the balance of grace, lions can see people as simply a means to an end, and as a result, can treat others with incredible insensitivity.

The beaver temperament can be so organized and methodical that it becomes legalistic. Again, just like the lion, the beaver has a tendency to value things over people. The standard of truth and order that beavers cherish becomes more important than the people around them. The budget mustn't bow to human pleas. The schedule cannot be changed to accommodate a broken heart. The process is the idol; the people are the worshippers. Thus, the beaver temperament without the balance of grace can be hard to live with.

On the other side of imbalance, both the otter and golden retriever temperaments have a tendency toward grace over truth. The otters are fun, spontaneous people. They are a party looking for a place to happen. However, they have a tendency to be shallow. Feeling a need for experience and fun, the otter can easily drop the standard of truth for the sake of enjoyment. Without meaning any harm, the otter can do much harm by operating without forethought and a commitment to absolute standards.

The golden retriever is another very relational temperament. In fact, this person is the most deeply relational of all the temperaments. Even though this makes for stability in relationships, it can also many times mean compromise of truth for the sake of people. The golden retriever, without the balance of truth, can render meaningless mercy to those around. The imbalanced golden retriever is often the enabler of the alcoholic, drug abuser, or otherwise destructive person. He or she is the shade tree from the heat of life many seek. However, without truth, one will perish in the shade of the golden retriever and sadly, so will the retriever.

In addition to the four basic temperaments, there are other

features that help to comprise our personalities such as our gender, our spiritual giftings, and so on. The main thing we must realize is that regardless of our strengths or giftings, any time we are functioning in an imbalance of truth and grace, we are relationally destructive. Regardless of the benefits and blessings of our strengths, they must be balanced by grace and truth to produce lasting results and to guard against damage.

grace truth

grace	truth
affection	rules
acceptance	discipline
praise	parameters
love	confrontation
forgiveness	objectivity
mercy	consequences
pursuit	Word of God

extreme grace is

naive
lacking superviston
littleor nodiscipline
permissive
without standards

extreme truth is

harsh/demanding
perfection!stic
authoitarian
critica/littleor nopraise
legalisti c

extreme grace produces

awrong concept of God...
   "He's apushove"
   "Heconl'ormstome."
   "Heis weak"
disrespect ofauthority
selfishness
confusi on
falsecomfort
deception
rejection *(theydon't (l)teenough
obouunerodisdplineme)*

extreme truth produces

a wrong concept of God...
   "Heisdistant."
   "Heisuncaring."
   "Heisharsh
low self-esteem
rebellion/resentment
anunhealthy drive to achieve
condennaion/self-hate
legalism
rejection*(Idon'trneasureup)*

The chart at left will help you see the ingredients of grace and truth and the results of extremes.

The Importance of Balance Related to Parenting

In raising children, the balance of grace and truth is critical. Here are three useful considerations for anyone with parenting responsibilities:

1. A Formula for Parenting

Rules + Relationship = Righteousness

If you raise your children with an equal emphasis on your relationship with them and the rules you expect them to obey, you will be able to produce the results you desire—a wholesome, healthy-minded young person. This is how God is with us. The relationship we have with Him is precious to Him. Also, the motivation and power we have to attain to His rules is His constant, personal presence in our lives.

When you separate rules from relationship, the formula changes:

Rules – Relationship = Rebellion

Many parents demand obedience from their children, but provide no supportive relationship. Children have a natural desire to spend time with their parents and to have fun with them. When requirements are put on a child combined with a withdrawal of parental relationship, the result will be either a hollow, forced obedience or just plain rebellion.

One other possible equation to our parenting formula is this:

Relationship – Rules = Destruction

Some parents are relational with their children, but don't provide rules.

An extreme example is a friend I had in the sixth grade. His mother let him and his younger brother smoke and drink around her. They were also exposed to a constant party atmosphere in their home as she and her live-in boyfriends practiced sin openly. By the time my friend was in high school, he had the physical appearance of an unhealthy man in his late twenties. Sin had taken its toll in his life.

2. Joe White's Teen Questionnaire

Joe White is the president of Kanakuk Kamps in Branson, Missouri. Every year, thousands of teenagers come to his popular Christian sports camps. He asks them this question: "What do you want most from your parents?" The number one response is surprising: *rules!* Clearly defined parameters are what teens want most from their parents. It makes them feel secure as it guards them from the tyranny of peer pressure and from having to find their own way.

The second most common answer to Joe's questionnaire shouldn't surprise you: *grace!* Yes, teens want grace. They want clearly defined parameters, but they also want them enforced within a family context of acceptance and forgiveness. By their own admission, teens want their parents to provide an atmosphere of grace and truth.

3. An Analogy of a Happy Family

A helpful word picture I once heard related to the family was this: *A successful family is a playground with a fence around it.* I really like that analogy, and I believe it carries a lot of truth.

A family should be fun, an organization of warmth and welcome for all of its members. The relationships we have with each other and the atmosphere of our homes should be built around enjoying God and each other. Through planned activities and prioritized relationships, our homes and family times become a sanctuary of enjoyment and encouragement—a playground, if you will.

To protect our family relationships as well as each individual in our families in their pursuits outside of the home, we must have parameters. Clearly defined rules protect each member and keep the atmosphere of our homes safe to enjoy. Thoughtful rules keep us from wandering into dangerous territory and keep dangerous territory from wandering into us. Therefore, clearly defined rules and parameters become a fence to protect our families.

A family of truth without grace is like a fence without a playground. It imprisons a soul without the benefit of relational inspiration. Even though it may be safe, it is also dead. A family of grace without truth is like a playground without a fence. Even though fun is allowed, it is constantly interrupted by the sounds of tragedy. Ultimately, all joy is stopped as destruction takes its inevitably heavy toll.

A successful family is a playground with a fence around it. It is a place of grace and truth in balance. It is the result of rules and relationship working in harmony to produce the desired goal. Just as God is full of grace and truth, so is the successful marriage and family life. It is one of the essential traits that makes us functional and happy.

To begin to see if your family atmosphere is balanced, check your concept of God. If you realize your view of God is imbalanced, accept what God's Word says and believe by faith in God's perfect character. After you examine your concept of God, the second place to look is at your home life while you were growing up. Were your parents

balanced? If your father was one extreme and your mother was another, that's not balance—that's confusion. If your parents were both at an extreme of grace or truth, it's just as bad and maybe worse.

Our parents' influence upon us is profound and even has a great effect on our concept of God. If your parents were imbalanced, forgive them and put your eyes on God. Also, if you realize you are making some of the same mistakes they made, confess it before God and your family and ask God to help you make the needed changes.

Another important step in bringing balance to your home is to look back at the chart earlier in this chapter. Look again at the components of grace and truth and see if any are missing in your home. If you realize some of the grace elements are missing, make it a priority to begin adding them. Also, if some of the truth issues are missing, do the same.

One final note. One of the surest ways you can recognize imbalance is by simply listening to the people around you. What does your spouse complain about? What are the issues he or she keeps bringing up? Do they represent a lack of grace or truth? Also, listen to your children and examine the fruits of your influence in their lives. If you will be willing to be open to God and people and let them speak into your life, you will be able to find balance.

Jesus is full of grace and truth. As a result, we are drawn to Him, and His influence in our lives is redemptive and powerful. The family full of grace and truth will also be a place where family members are drawn. In addition, the function of a balanced family will be redemptive and powerful. It will be a place of lasting joy and loving progress. Also, like God Himself, the family full of grace and truth is invincible and eternal.

Let not mercy and truth forsake you;
Bind them around your neck,
Write them on the tablet of your heart,
And so find favor and high esteem
In the sight of God and man.
Proverbs 3:3–4

SECRET THREE

Healthy Dependency

In this day and time when we hear so much about personal independence, we need to be reminded of one thing: God created mankind to be dependent beings. Each one of us is dependent because God created us that way. The ultimate perversion of God's creation is independence. First of all, personal independence is a deception. Secondly, it is a perversion of God's plan. God has designed our lives with an inherent dependence that operates on three levels.

1. We are dependent upon God.

All through the Bible, mankind is compared to sheep. Since the Scriptures are divinely inspired, we need to understand what God means when He compares us to sheep. Sheep are cuddly-looking animals, but they are beset with weaknesses and limitations. They are absolutely vulnerable as it relates to being able to protect themselves. They have no sharp hooves or sharp teeth, and they are not aggressive.

They also have no navigational equipment. Unlike homing pigeons, whales, or other migratory animals that have the ability to wander hundreds or even thousands of miles and find their way back, sheep can't travel any significant distance without help. They also cannot provide for themselves. They're not hunters; therefore, they lack the predatory skills they need to gather food independently.

So, when God looks at us and says, "You're My sheep," what does He mean? In essence, He is saying, "I created you without the ability to get where you're going. You need Me. I created you without the ability to provide for yourself. You need Me." Isaiah 40:11 puts it well:

> *"He will feed His flock like a shepherd; He will gather the lambs with His arm, and carry them in His bosom, and gently lead those who are with young."*

Jesus refers to Himself as the Good Shepherd, and He declares His willingness to lay down His life for us.

The life of a person who has understood and accepted his or her weakness and has turned to Christ for guidance, protection, and provision is a life of incredible blessing and fullness. Probably the best description of the life dependent upon God was written by David in Psalm 23:1,

> *"The Lord is my shepherd; I shall not want."*

Human nature is such that we believe we can make it on our own. It is the reason Satan was able to lead Adam and Eve into rebellion. Simply put, we hate being dependent upon God. It's part of our fallen nature. The prophet Isaiah said it best:

> *"All we like sheep have gone astray; we have turned, every one, to his own way; and the Lord has laid on Him the iniquity of us all"*
> Isaiah 53:6

To take this truth even further, human sin is an independent spirit. Yet, the more mature we become in Christ, the healthier we become, and the more we accept the fact that we are dependent upon

God. In fact, the essence of successful Christianity is a daily dependence upon the Lord for all of our significant needs. The prayerful, trusting believer has accepted his or her dependence upon Christ and has learned to trust in Him daily as a faithful shepherd.

2. We are dependent upon the opposite sex.

Not only does it take both man and woman to propagate human life, but both are also necessary in order to reflect the fullness of God's endowment upon humanity. God has given men special abilities and perspectives women don't have. God has also endowed women with special traits and sensitivities, which are lacking in men. When men and women respect each other and share their unique gifts with one another as God designed, we are both benefited and blessed.

The so-called "battle of the sexes" is based upon generations of frustration and tension between men and women. Through misunderstandings, abuse, and rejection, many men and women have learned to protect themselves from each other. In some extreme instances, some have even gone so far as to completely reject the opposite sex and to plan them out of their lives.

Regardless of how much tension or frustration exists in one's life related to the opposite sex, we must realize that we need each other. It is God's design. Learning to understand and accept our God-given differences and using them to complement each other in a divine interdependence is one of the most important keys to social stability and emotional health. Surely, the proper function of every marriage and family relies on a peaceful and trusting interaction between the sexes.

3. We are dependent upon the Body of Christ.

The twelfth chapter of I Corinthians tells us that the Holy Spirit distributes giftings in the Church to everyone as He wishes. According to Paul's writing, no person is left ungifted in the Church, and no person is given all of the gifts. The Holy Spirit sovereignly divides the giftings of God throughout the Body of Christ. The result is a fully gifted Church that is able to express the manifold ministry of Christ within itself and to the world. As a whole, we are complete.

Individually, we are incomplete and dependent upon the larger Body for perspective, ability, and wholeness.

When I was called into the ministry, I felt helpless to prepare myself and to get where God wanted me to be. Even though God was faithful to guide me every step of the way and to provide every resource throughout my journey, He used my brothers and sisters in Christ as His primary means to fulfill His call for me. When I look back on how many people invested in my life to get me where I am today, I am humbled and thankful. Without a doubt, if Karen and I had been isolated from healthy Christian fellowship, we wouldn't have made it.

God has designed His Body, the Church, in such a way as to force us to depend upon one another. Not only has He given all of us giftings that represent a part of His own ministry and mindset, but He has also withheld a part of the relationship He has with us so that we cannot gain directly from Christ what He has designed that we receive from fellowship with other believers.

In other words, we cannot refuse intimate Christian fellowship and not suffer. Independence is punished by a lack of divine nourishment and spiritual deposit in essential areas of our lives. If we want to live in the fullness of Christ, dependence upon the Body of Christ is a must. Part of what Christ will reveal to us and provide for us, He will manifest through the flesh-and-blood relationships we have with fellow believers, or He won't do it at all. Once again, His design is respectful, relational dependence.

In understanding our basic dependence upon God, the opposite sex and the Body of Christ, it's also important that we understand the dynamics that make dependencies work properly and the parameters that keep them from becoming unhealthy and dysfunctional. There are four important rules concerning dependence that keep it healthy and functional.

Four Rules for Healthy Dependency

Rule #1: Our primary dependence must be upon God.

Let's look further into the healthy dependencies God has created in us and for us. The example of the Samaritan woman who met Jesus at the well illustrates the dysfunctional condition we risk when we fail to trust primarily in God. Here is what the Bible says about her enlightening encounter with Jesus:

A woman of Samaria came to draw water. Jesus said to her, "Give Me a drink." For His disciples had gone away into the city to buy food.
Then the woman of Samaria said to Him, "How is it that you, being a Jew, ask a drink from me, a Samaritan woman?" For Jews have no dealings with Samaritans. Jesus answered and said to her, "If you knew the gift of God, and who it is who says to you, 'Give Me a drink,' you would have asked Him, and He would have given you living water."
John 4:7–10

Puzzled at the very least by the Lord's remark, or reacting purely in the natural, the woman questioned Jesus further. She knew the well was very deep and wondered how He could draw the "living water." Did He have powers greater than Jacob who drank from the well himself, watered his livestock there, and quenched the thirst of his sons? In His exchange with the Samaritan woman, Jesus clarified the real meaning of what He was offering.

Jesus answered and said to her, "Whoever drinks of this water will thirst again, but whoever drinks of the water that I shall give him will never thirst. But the water that I shall give him will become in him a fountain of water springing up into everlasting life."
John 4:13– 14

It was an appealing, life-giving offer the Samaritan woman herself couldn't refuse. It was reinforced all the more by Jesus' supernatural knowledge that the woman had experienced five failed marriages and was now living with a man who was not her husband.

In the Jewish culture of the day, this spiritually thirsty individual had at least three strikes against her. A woman, she ranked no higher than property, a man's chattel. A Samaritan, she was despised by the Jews. An adulteress, she lived a life of sin-riddled scandal. Not realizing she had encountered the Lord of lords, she was shocked by the compassion of the man she met at Jacob's well.

She wondered why He would even speak to her, why He would ask her for a drink. And yet, if she had only understood in whose awesome presence she stood and the profound relationship He was offering, she would have asked Him for the drink, only to have her thirst quenched for eternity.

Jesus didn't stand by the well to judge the woman. He was there to heal her. His heart of compassion poured out to her as it does to us today in all of our brokenness. His cup of living water is offered to broken marriages, broken families, broken lives.

The Samaritan woman was depending upon relationships with people, primarily men, to meet her deepest needs. She was trying to fill the void in her life with something and someone else—a void only Christ could fill. The result was a trail of failure and disappointment in her life and a still present inner thirst that had never been quenched. Her dilemma is common for humanity. Most of us, even most Christians, are tempted to take the tangible people and things around us that offer satisfaction and fulfillment and to use them to replace God.

This is the reason Jesus told her that if she continued to drink from the well of natural water, she would continue to thirst. He was trying to get her focus off of the worldly level onto a spiritual, eternal level. He was also trying to get her to understand the limits of natural and human provision.

Primary dependence upon the tangible things and people around us to meet our deepest inner needs will end up in failure, hurt, and cynicism. It is interesting that after five bad marriages, the Samaritan woman had now given up on marriage and was living with a man.

The moral of this story is that only God can meet our deepest needs. When our primary dependence is upon God, not only does He fill the inner void in our lives with His love and rich presence, but He also flows out of us to others. This is why Jesus told the Samaritan woman that the water He would give her would become a "fountain of water springing up."

Not only are we enriched and blessed by God's provision, but it also makes a dramatic impact upon the lives of those around us. Literally, the most loving act you will ever perform for yourself and your family is to seek and serve Jesus Christ. Not only will He transform you internally in areas where material and human resources can never reach, but He also will prepare you to love as you have never loved before.

The Samaritan woman was a person who was hopelessly lost in a world that had promised her love and had relentlessly disappointed and rejected her. Jesus came to repair her and heal her. In so doing, He addressed the root of the problem—a void in her life that only He could fill. As the ultimate marriage and relationship counselor, Jesus approached a woman who would cause the best earthly counselor to grab a textbook and pray hard.

It is interesting that His help for her didn't directly address her relational problems from a technical perspective. In other words, Jesus didn't focus on the do's and don'ts of how to love a man. He focused on the lack of internal enablement in her life because of the spiritual void within her.

I believe the primary cause for the marriage and family problems in America today is this issue. Because we are a materialistic culture that has largely replaced God with our own answers, we are suffering the consequences of failed relationships, emotional trauma, and social cynicism. Even though we may not think we have much in common with the Samaritan woman, we bear a striking resemblance to her relationally and spiritually.

The answer for us today is the same as it was for her. We must stop making our primary source a human, natural source and turn to Jesus first to meet our deepest inner needs. His promise is that if we will come to Him and drink from His well daily, we will "never thirst again." What an incredible promise!

Matthew 6:33 says it another way:

*"But seek first the kingdom of God and His righteousness, and all of
these things shall be added to you."*

In this verse, Jesus promises that if we will turn our hearts toward
Him and seek Him, He will faithfully meet our needs on every level
of life. Not only does a life of seeking the Lord result in inner
blessing, but it also means a life of peace and provision for our
economic, social, and practical needs. The impact that a life turned
toward Christ has upon family relationships is immeasurable. For
your sake and the sake of those you love, open your heart to the Lord
and seek Him daily.

**Rule #2: Our secondary dependence is upon equal or greater
relationships.**

Understanding that our most important dependency is upon
God, we then need to recognize our need for equal or greater
relationships. These relationships are characterized by an ability to
relate on a social, emotional, and practical level that gives us pleasure
and fulfillment. These relationships include spouses, friends,
spiritual leaders, extended family, work associates, teachers, and
other relationships of this type. Of course, related to the average
family, the most important relationship on this level is with our
spouses.

As spouses, we need to depend upon each other to build a
relationship of deep trust and mutual support. This interdependence
is very important for the development of intimacy and the fulfillment
of the needs of both spouses. It also provides a strong foundation for
parenting. The unity and cooperation of a couple create a healthy
environment for them to parent their children and a secure
environment for them to develop.

In every marriage relationship, there are problems to work
through and obstacles to overcome in developing and maintaining
deep trust and intimacy. We must never give up in our search for
harmony in marriage. The temptation to give up isn't just a danger to

our marriages; it dramatically impacts other areas of our lives as well. Also, in giving up on our spouses, we will automatically turn the dependence we had on them to something else, creating even further frustration, hurt, and dysfunction. Couples must strive to keep their relationships healthy and growing. Regardless of the price, the benefits are worth it; and the consequences for not doing so are just too high.

In addition to our relationships with our spouses, we also need a group of godly, supportive friends. These friendships should never interfere with our relationship with God or our family, but they should be committed relationships that give us the ability to relate in a healthy environment of exchange. Any close friendships we have should be with fellow believers who share our same values. We should develop and maintain friendships with people who support us in following God and maintaining the health and priority of our marriages and families. These relationships are extremely important.

Over the years of pastoring and counseling people concerning their marriages and families, I have noticed a common thread among those who constantly struggle and eventually fail in family relationships; they have either no godly, supportive relationships around them and/or they are involved in unhealthy relationships that are unsupportive and even competitive with Biblical family values. I Corinthians 15:33 says this: *"Do not be deceived: 'Evil company corrupts good habits.'"*

We must diligently strive to build and maintain healthy friendships. The best place to build these types of relationships is through a healthy, Bible-based church. If you aren't involved in one, find one. If you are involved in one, stay involved. Don't remain on the fringes. Through your involvement, you will be able to meet and build relationships with healthy people. There is no such thing as a perfect person, Christian or non-Christian. However, when a person is committed to following God and living by the standards of Scripture, his or her influence on us will be healthy. Individually, as a couple, and as a family, we need these relationships.

We also need to find accountability and support from spiritual authority, such as our pastors and other spiritual leaders. There are many times in our lives when we need outside, objective input. We can gain this on a weekly basis by being involved in worship services and small groups such as Sunday school classes and Bible studies. We can also gain this at special times through personal counseling with a leader or pastor. These relationships are an important link to keep us on the right track and to keep emotional and volatile personal issues from harming us and our families.

I have described what is a healthy reliance on our spouses, friends, and authority figures. Here are two common and very dangerous violations regarding dependency in relationships. These two mistakes are a perversion of God's design and always create dysfunction when they are present.

Parent-to-Child Dependency

The family structure of God's design finds the child relying on his or her parents and the parents meeting the needs of the child. It is a perversion of God's plan when the parent is dependent on the child, and years of emotional abuse are set up within that type of family structure.

Understand that I'm not referring to the older parent who becomes incapacitated for some reason and relies on assistance from an adult child. It is perfectly appropriate for us to care for our aging parents when that time comes. What I am referring to is the dangerous scenario of school-aged children and even younger ones in the home meeting the needs of the parents.

Here's one way that scene is played out in modern times: We find teenagers getting pregnant because they want someone to love them. A young teenage girl will bring a baby into the world and expect this child to make her feel loved and special. She expects that son or daughter to always be there for her. Instead, she raises a victim of emotional abuse who is virtually certain to perpetuate the dysfunction on into the next generation.

You cannot expect your children to fix what is wrong with you!

Depending on a child to prop you up is called "triangling." The worst part of triangling is that it stunts the child's emotional development. Long before the child is equipped physically, psychologically, or spiritually, he or she is forced to become a parent to the parent. Often, such children shoulder the responsibility for maintaining a peaceful equilibrium around the house or for keeping their parents emotionally healthy and together. They commonly accept the blame when their efforts fail; and by the time they grow up, they're broken, relationally impaired human beings in need of deep inner healing.

When children are put in the position of having to emotionally prop up their parents, they cannot properly develop as children. Children need to be children, and adults need to be adults. Children should not have to "fix" adults. It is not God's design.

Now, picture the family with two or more children, one of whom is used to meet the parents' emotional needs. Two types of children come out of that family: the favored child with whom the parents bond in an unhealthy way, and the non-favored child who is out of the emotional loop. The favored child cannot develop properly, and the non-favored child feels unloved and unwanted because he or she is not as special as the brother or sister who is close to their mother and father—another disastrous outcome of unhealthy dependencies in a family!

When children leave a home where they've been the emotional prop for their parents, the parents lose a sense of security. Often, they then pursue the children into adulthood and into their own marriages. Many times parents become adversarial with their children's spouses because they are competing for love and attention.

A lady I know told me her own sad story. Her mother moved into her marriage to dominate and control everything she could, just as she had done early in this woman's life. She and her husband finally moved over a thousand miles away hoping to free themselves from her mother. As a result, her mother sued them for grandparent's visitation rights, and the couple spent over eighteen thousand dollars to fight her in court.

This woman's mother was trying to fill a void in her life through her children and grandchildren. Her behavior produced incredible damage to her family. Rather than accepting responsibility for her behavior, she instead chose to blame her child and to insist on further emotional access. This woman is extremely abusive and wrong. She needs to find her primary fulfillment in God and in her relationships with her husband and friends. An absence of significance and fulfillment in these areas is a common trait of problem in-laws.

Parent-to-child dependency also creates sexual confusion. A little girl needs her father, but she needs more of her mother. A little boy needs his mother, but he needs more of his father. We need same-sex identification. When a mother looks to her son for emotional support, or a father props himself up on his daughter, sexual confusion often results. This is called "cross-gender triangling," and I believe it is a major cause of homosexuality.

A precious, gifted Christian man came to me once, admitting he had been struggling with homosexuality for years. He said, "My father was a traveling salesman, and I rarely saw him. We had no relationship. My mother was my best friend. From the time I was a young child, all I remember is my mother coming to me to confide in me and talk with me about her personal issues. There was nothing that she wouldn't do in front of me. So, when I became eleven or twelve years old and I began to have sexual feelings, females weren't the opposite sex for me; males were."

When a child enters puberty and becomes interested in the opposite sex, there should be a mystique about them. There should be an attraction as between opposite magnetic forces. Whenever there has been an improper cross-gender triangling, the child is unhealthily bonded to the opposite sex. This causes even greater problems when the child has had little or no bonding to the parent of the same sex. The common result is an unhealthy mystique and attraction created for the same sex. It is very critical that as parents we love our children aggressively and faithfully, but not use them to fulfill us emotionally.

Triangling children also causes them to be mistrained for their marriage and family relationships later on. How can our children succeed unless we give them a model of success? God has put us in our children's lives to be role models for them. We need to show them our dependency upon God. Parents praying together isn't just a nice little scene in a Christian picture. Parents praying together is critical in everyday family living to show our children that we trust in Jesus.

Jesus is here to help us overcome our problems. Jesus is here to give us direction in our lives. Our children need to know that we trust in the Lord. Then, they need to know Mom and Dad trust in each other, talk to each other, and pray with each other. It is also very important for children to see their parents show affection for one another as well as to receive it personally.

In homes where the parents don't have a relationship with God or each other, the children often become objects of the parents' dependence. They grow up to perpetuate the dysfunction in their own homes as adults because they learned that model of behavior as they grew up. Persons raised in abusive families, alcoholic families, materialistic families, or emotionally dysfunctional families many times struggle throughout life trying to overcome the modeling that took place in their lives when they were growing up. My appeal to parents is to deal with your needs and problems in a mature and godly manner. Following the first two rules of dependency means that when you are faced with needs and difficulties in life, you turn to God or an equal or greater relationship, but never to your children.

Non-Relational Dependency

When things become factors of dependency in a person's life or when they start to take the place of a healthy relationship with God and others, a whole hornet's nest of dysfunction develops. What kind of things?

- Alcohol
- Drugs
- Food

- Money
- Success
- Acquisitions
- Pornography

The danger of using things for dependency is that they lead us away from relationship with God and with our families. In many cases, they actually replace God and family in our lives. Because we turn to a substance or thing, talking or praying isn't necessary. The substance fixes and fills us, at least for a few minutes, and so an inevitable dependency is built up to the point that the thing we are dependent upon becomes an essential fixture in our lives.

In Matthew, chapter 22, Jesus tells us the top two commandments of God. The first is that we love God with all of our hearts, souls, minds, and strength. The second great commandment is that we love our neighbor as ourselves. It is obvious by Jesus' words that God and people are to be the focus of our lives. This is where we are to turn for strength, fulfillment, and love.

The relationships we have should never be replaced by an inanimate object or medication. If we allow this to happen, not only will we experience relational problems with God and man, but we will also be stuck in a dead end of addiction and emptiness. Even though substances and things promise great security and comfort, they provide very little, and the price they exact from us is high.

If you are currently using things as a replacement for God and people, I want to encourage you to be honest and get help. First of all, turn to God and open your heart to Him. He loves you just the way you are and will lovingly accept you as you turn toward Him and trust Him to heal you and fill you. Also, turn to the people around you for support. In addition to family members, find a Christian support group that can help you deal with what you are going through. This principle is powerful, and it applies to all of us. It is a well-documented fact that people who trust and depend on relationships with others are far more successful than people who don't.

Rule #3: Dependency must not diminish or usurp personal responsibility.

To draw together what has been discussed so far, we need to remember that the first rule of dependency is that we must trust in God first. After that, the second rule of dependency is that we depend upon equal or greater relationships. That brings us to the third rule: dependency must not diminish or usurp personal responsibility.

Personal responsibility is very important. As you will read later on in this book, the issue of being responsible for our own behavior is one of the most foundational doctrines in Scripture. God created us with a free will and holds us responsible for the decisions we make. Therefore, in life we must learn to make our decisions with prayer and forethought. Also, regardless of the relationships in which we are involved, we are responsible for our own decisions. Dependency upon others must never transgress the boundaries of our free will or be used to replace our personal decision making.

An example of this issue is spiritual abuse. It is a real danger because it replaces God with religious leaders. This is convenient for many people because human leaders are more tangible than God and are most often more than happy to provide direction. Abusive spiritual leaders aren't abusive because they help provide direction for people. They are abusive because they usurp God's personal authority as well as interfere with an individual's personal decision making. Abusive spiritual leaders impose upon people with their strong desire to represent God and repress personal volition.

As a pastor, I must be very careful not to replace God in people's lives. I am particularly sensitive to people who are insecure and those who put leaders on a pedestal. These types of people often want a person to tell them what to do. Unfortunately, these precious people are prey for spiritual abuse because they are willing to surrender to someone else their personal responsibility to make their own decisions.

Some do this because they are insecure and feel as though the spiritual leader is more qualified to direct their lives. Others do this because they have the distorted concept that a spiritual leader is equal to God. Therefore, to question the direction that is set is equal to sin against God. Spiritually abusive leaders almost always accompany their message and ministry with the threat that any questioning or rebellion will be punished by God.

The responsibility of a godly leader is to point people toward the Lord and to help people build their knowledge and skills of how to live life successfully. Never should a spiritual leader dominate or begin to control another's personal life. Even though for some people it might be convenient to have someone else make decisions for them, it is wrong and will always lead to harm and dysfunction.

As odd as it may seem, there are many people who don't want to make their own decisions. Many men and women in prison today are there because they choose that environment rather than life on the outside. In prison, they are told when to wake up, when to go to sleep, when to eat, etc. Therefore, they live a regimented life with very little personal responsibility. Their prison becomes more internal than external.

Other men and women choose to live in a prison in their homes. They live with a person who dominates them, tells them what to do, and rules the relationship. Why do they allow it? Even though almost every person resents being dominated, many put up with it because they don't want to have to make their own decisions and stand up for themselves.

They weigh the negatives of emotional abuse and domination with the pressures created by having to make decisions for themselves, and they choose abuse. This scenario is responsible for a great deal of dysfunction in homes. Until the weaker, dominated spouse begins to stand up in love and challenge the dominating mate, the dysfunction won't stop.

Sickness is another element that usurps personal responsibility. Even though all of us become sick at times, there are some people who love to be sick or say they are sick because they don't want to be responsible. Being well means that you have to care for yourself and others. Being sick means others take care of you. In the fifth chapter of the Gospel of John, there is the story of a man who had been sick at the Pool of Bethesda for thirty-eight years. Jesus walked up to him one day and asked him if he wanted to be well.

That might seem like a silly question, but Jesus asked it because it was at the root of why the man had been at the pool for so long.

I knew a lady who was chronically ill all of her adult life. As soon as they treated one of her illnesses, she began to complain of a new one. She was medicated and treated all of her adult life. The interesting thing was that she was never really ill. Even the doctors said that her complaints were mostly unfounded.

She was as social as she wanted to be; however, when anything was demanded of her or caused her to be responsible, she immediately pulled out a major illness as an excuse. Every member of her family and all of her friends knew she was a hypochondriac. Her behavior created deep resentment in her husband and children and produced dysfunction in their home.

Rather than using sickness as a crutch, we need to turn to God as a cure. Rather than retreating into a world of defeat, we need to accept God's gift of power to overcome our fears and weaknesses. Through His loving power, we are given the resources to overcome. If you struggle with this issue, be honest before God and others and make up your mind that you are going to take responsibility to face life with the help of God and His people.

Rule #4: Dependency must not interfere with a greater dependence.

If you are a parent, this rule means you don't usurp God's place in your child's life, especially as the child grows older. If you are a pastor or spiritual leader, this means you lead people constantly to a greater understanding and dependence upon the Lord, not on yourself. It is common for parents and people in authority to cause an unhealthy dependence upon themselves that violates a greater dependence.

Another example of this is our involvement with our married friends. As much as you may love and enjoy the friendship of some other couples you know, be careful never to interfere with their marriages. Be there for them as friends, pray with them, and provide them with godly counsel if asked, but never try to interfere with or replace someone's spouse. If you notice that the couple or one person in the marriage is depending upon you too much, you need to say to them in a loving way, "You both need to be with each other more, and I need to be with you less."

Also, don't spring to the defense of one married person over his or her spouse unless there is something criminal involved. Chances are you'll never know the full story until you have talked to both parties and prayed. Therefore, the best you can do is to pray for them and let them work out their own problems without your involvement. This may be difficult to do sometimes, but your friend's marriage is a higher priority than you are, and you need to honor that. When your friends are offended at their mates or are just depending on you too much, you must direct them home and not allow their dependence upon you to violate their marriage bond.

We are dependent people—dependent upon God, the opposite sex, and our brothers and sisters in Christ. We are also dependent, in the human sense, upon many different abilities and resources of the people around our neighborhoods, our country, and even around the world. The fact that we are dependent is obvious. To deny this is arrogance and deception.

However, in accepting our dependency, there are other deceptions and pitfalls that can sabotage our hopes for happiness and fulfillment in life. Every dysfunctional family is to some degree an example of distorted, misplaced dependency. They are in that condition because they have broken the rules. For any of us who may be in this condition today, if we will simply acknowledge our shortcomings and transfer the expectations of our needs to the correct source within the correct parameters, the result will be a fulfilling, successful life.

> *Ho! Everyone who thirsts, come to the waters; and you who have*
> *no money, come, buy and eat. Yes, come, buy wine and milk*
> *without money and without price. Why do you spend money for*
> *what is not bread, and your wages for what does not satisfy? Listen*

carefully to Me, and eat what is good, and let your soul delight itself
in abundance.
Isaiah 55:1–2

Jesus answered and said to her, "Whoever drinks of this water will
thirst again, but whoever drinks of the water that I shall give him
will never thirst. But the water that I shall give him will become in
him a fountain of water springing up into everlasting life."
John 4:13– 14

SECRET FOUR

Positive Communication

Happy, successful families talk. They have the ability to communicate and to work through their problems. Dysfunctional families either don't talk, won't talk, or they talk in the wrong way. One of the most important factors determining the health of marriage and family relationships is good communication and the ability to resolve conflicts in a positive manner.

Communication is a critical skill for couples and families. One of the most important benefits of healthy communication in family life is intimacy. Intimacy cannot be developed without healthy communication. One of the primary factors of falling in love and growing deeper and closer in a relationship is a positive exchange of words. Through words, hearts and minds connect together.

Understanding the importance of communication, Satan does all he can to attack this important area. He knows that if he can prohibit or poison the words between us, he can ruin our relationships. This is exactly what he attempts to do. He realizes that if he can infiltrate and break our lines of communication, he can destroy our families or at the very least damage them. His mission is to take loving, intimate relationships and turn them into wastelands of hurt and confusion.

Another issue related to the importance of communication is that it is one of our deepest needs. In marriage seminars, I teach about the four major needs of men and women. One of a woman's most profound needs is the need for open and honest communication. A husband's meeting this need in his wife is essential for the proper functioning of the marriage and the bonding of their relationship. Even though communication may not rank in the top four of men's needs, it is nevertheless important in their lives. I once thought I didn't need communication, except on a superficial level. However, when I started meeting Karen's need in this area, I began to enjoy it and desire it as much as she did, and it took our marriage to a higher level than we had ever been.

Communication is also a profound need in our children's lives. Children need their parents to talk to them. They need positive words flowing into their lives. They need their parents to answer their questions and share openly with them. They need to be affirmed, trained, and informed on a daily basis. Healthy communication between parents and children creates a bond between them and allows the parents to communicate values, direction, and discipline in a healthy way. However, when communication is unhealthy or lacking, children pay the price.

The Power of Communication

Words are very powerful. Because of this, the Bible is full of directives concerning the manner in which we communicate. In Matthew 12:36–37, Jesus warns,

> *"But I say to you that for every idle word men may speak, they will give account of it in the day of judgment. For by your words you will be justified, and by your words you will be condemned."*

This Scripture surprises a lot of people because they think that words can be used casually without consequence. According to the Bible, what we say—every significant and every idle word—is recorded in heaven and will be used to judge us eternally. Of course, when we repent of sins, they are forgiven and erased. However, when we don't repent, there are serious consequences to be faced in this life and in eternity.

Another very significant Scripture related to the power of communication is Proverbs 18:21. It says,

"Death and life are in the power of the tongue, and those who love it will eat its fruit."

All of us know the pain we have experienced by the words someone has spoken to us. In fact, some of the deepest wounds we can experience come from the careless, insensitive speech of the people close to us. Many people live in families where words are used to hurt and destroy. Sarcasm, criticism, verbal abuse, shame, and anger all manifest themselves as negative forces that kill relationships.

As easily as words can kill, they can also bring life. The words of our mouths can encourage, heal, bless, and communicate love and affection. The choice is ours, moment by moment. Satan loves nothing more than to turn a house into a verbal war zone. He takes two people who once spoke nothing but kind, affectionate words to one another and gradually turns them into verbal terrorists. Not only do they suffer, but their children are also greatly affected by their negative communication.

Healthy, positive communication begins when we understand the incredible power of every single word we speak. Once we have done this, we then must submit our mouths to the Lord and dedicate them to being vessels for Him to speak through. Literally, the mouth that produces a successful, healthy marriage and family is one that is led by the Lord.

As we submit to the Lord and ask the Holy Spirit to help us learn to communicate, our language is transformed into a praising, healing, loving fountain of life. Our words are meant to give life to our relationships. The successful family is a family with an understanding of this issue. Its members have submitted themselves to the Lord and stay accountable to God and one another for the way they communicate.

The first chapter of Genesis says that God created the world with His words. To a large degree, you also create your world with your words. Your marriage and family world is created with your words. I can tell you this with confidence: if you have a good marriage, there are good words being exchanged between you. If you have a happy family, then there are positive words being exchanged among you.

I can also promise you this: if you have a bad marriage, there are either few words or unhealthy words spoken between you. If you have a hurting, dysfunctional family, there are either no words or negative words being exchanged. Words play a powerful role in dictating the atmosphere of our lives. Whether we realize it or not, words have a creative force behind them. Therefore, we must be careful about what we say because we will live with the results, good or bad.

Another Scripture that speaks of the power of communication comes from the book of James. He paints a vivid mental picture of the influence our words play in directing our lives. James 3:4 likens the tongue to a small rudder that steers a mighty ship. According to James, our tongues determine the direction of our lives. Even though the rudder of a ship might seem insignificant and not be one of the most notable features of the vessel, everything on the ship is dependent upon the rudder to get where it is going.

This is true of communication. Even though it might not be something we think about a lot, the words we speak to each other in our marriages and families dictate where we are going. Regardless of how insignificant we might think it is, every area of family life is dependent upon healthy communication for success.

Six Traits of Destructive Communication

One of the ways we can begin to better our family communication is by learning to identify unhealthy communication traits. Many of us have adopted destructive forms of communication from our childhood experiences. Especially if we grew up in homes where there was unhealthy communication, we are more prone to having problems and repeating the patterns of our past. Even if we weren't raised in a significantly dysfunctional environment, it is still important for us to understand negative communication traits so we can avoid them. The six common destructive communication traits are as follows:

1. **Silence**—Rather than talking about issues and resolving them relationally, many people use silence to both punish and intimidate their spouses and families. At the first sign of tension or conflict, the healthy thing to do is to sit down and talk things out before things get out of hand. This becomes even more important where anger is present. The sooner it is brought out into the open and disarmed, the better.

Silence in a marriage and family is a dangerous thing. It is not only a non-relational, antisocial form of behavior, but it is also a guarantee of prolonged problems. Many adults I counsel who have experienced lifelong emotional problems and pain come from homes where one or both parents used silence to punish and control.

2. **Verbal Abuse**— It is not unusual for people to live in homes where cursing, name-calling, and verbal intimidation are common. "You're stupid." "You idiot, you'll never amount to anything." "You're the black sheep of the family." "I wish you were never born." "I'm going to beat the_ out of you if you don't straighten up," etc. These are all examples of verbal abuse.

There are two basic levels of verbal abuse in families. The first is between spouses—husbands and wives who get in fights and begin to scream, curse, name-call, and belittle each other. In some cases, the verbal abuse is even accompanied by physical abuse. Not only is it extremely damaging for spouses to speak to each other this way, but it is also very harmful to the children to hear their parents speaking negatively to each other.

One of parents' most important roles is to train their children in proper communication and conflict resolution. The reason there is so much youth violence on our streets and in our schools today is because there is so much hostility at home. In many cases, young people are simply resolving conflict the same way they see it done at home.

The second level of verbal abuse is between parent and child. Children need patient guidance and loving discipline. A caring parent who uses praise and positive support is God's design for raising children. When our children willfully disobey us, we should use consistent, fair, and loving discipline to correct them. Many parents who are preoccupied with something else expect their children to obey and perform without investment and training from the parent. Their substitute for patient training is verbal assault. Using name-calling, shame, intimidation, and cursing, these parents try to produce through verbal bullying what they should be producing through careful nurturing.

3. Manipulation—I know a woman who couldn't conceive children, and it was breaking her heart. Her doctor said there was no medical reason why she couldn't conceive. When we began to talk about some of the events in her life, she related something that happened when she was a little girl. Her mother caught her doing something wrong one day and said to her, "Because you've done that, you'll never be able to have children." This mother literally put a curse on her daughter with her words, and it was physically causing the daughter not to be able to conceive. I explained to her that this type of behavior was not of God. We prayed, breaking that curse over her in the name of Jesus; she became pregnant and bore children.

Many parents and spouses use verbal manipulation to control one another and get their way. Manipulation is the use of dishonesty, partial truth, or truth for the purpose of one's own advantage. The main feature of manipulation is selfishness. Rather than an honest, humble conversation for the betterment of everyone involved, manipulation seeks to tilt the scales toward itself without revealing its true motive. A relationship built around manipulation is a tangled web of mistrust, dishonesty, and exploitation.

4. Erratic and Inconsistent Behavior— In a dysfunctional home, one day you're an angel; the next day you're the devil. All of us have days that are better than others. However, in dysfunctional families, the parents, or maybe just one parent, goes from Dr. Jekyll to Mr. Hyde. One day the world is great, the mood is good, and positive things are being said. The next day, the mood may be bad, and angry words are spouted, perhaps even a tongue-lashing takes place. Spouses and children don't know what to expect in this type of home. An atmosphere of insecurity and mistrust prevails in this unpredictable, moody environment.

We must be careful in our relationships to be consistent in communication. I have counseled many married couples who have experienced a breakdown of communication only to find the root cause is that one spouse has closed up because of hurt feelings and mistrust. One particular husband I counseled told me that he had learned not to expose himself emotionally to his wife, because as soon as her mood changed, her spirit became mean and hurtful. Even though she couldn't understand why he had grown so withdrawn and distant, her moody, inconsistent behavior was the cause.

It is also important that our children are raised in an environment of consistency. Regardless of how we feel, we need to build a positive atmosphere in our marriage and family relationships. If something is bothering us, we need to deal with it in a healthy way and not take it out on everyone. Also, if we aren't feeling well physically, we need to be honest about it and seek to get well. However, sickness isn't an excuse for meanness and selfishness.

5. Dishonesty— Family communication must, above all other things, be honest. This doesn't mean a graphic, insensitive honesty about everything we know. It does mean that we speak the truth and deal with reality. For spouses, this means not denying our problems and not withholding emotionally from one another. Honesty is essential in building harmony and intimacy and also in resolving conflicts.

As it relates to parenting, children need someone to talk with concerning their fears, hurts, and questions. Many parents use dishonesty to try to dispel children's emotions or answer their questions. Dishonesty related to family problems, sex, God, and sensitive issues doesn't help a child; it simply places the child in a false environment on a road leading to disappointment, frustration, and failure. The reason some parents are dishonest is because they take the easy way out of a situation. The reason others are dishonest is because they are living in denial themselves. They are giving their children the answer they are trying to convince themselves is true. A family based on denial and dishonesty is a house of smoke and mirrors that will eventually collapse.

6. Secret Keeping— All of us have confidential issues that need to be kept within the family. However, if there is destruction in your family, you need to tell someone and get help. When there is sexual abuse, spouse abuse, child abuse, or any illegal or destructive behavior within a family, someone needs to go for outside help. Either a friend, a spiritual leader, or sometimes even the police may need to be called to intervene in a situation.

Many children who come out of dysfunctional, abusive homes were told or even threatened never to tell anyone what was happening. These children experienced or witnessed anything from severe violence to sexual molestation. However, they were locked in a virtual prison because of an unhealthy obligation to keep the dark secrets of the family.

Successful families honor confidentiality, but they don't cover up destruction. If we are the victims of abuse or witness destructive or illegal behavior in our families—we need to understand that real love reaches out and gets help. We should never demand of our family members that they allow us to self-destruct or destroy others while they cover for us. We should love each other enough in our families to keep confidentiality, but to expose abuse and destruction for the sake of the family.

In speaking of these six traits of destructive communication, I realize that some people can identify with all of these. However, most of us can identify with one or two. If you can identify with any of these traits, it's probable that you came from a home that modeled unhealthy communication to you. The first step to being free from problems stemming from your past is to recognize the problems and to be honest about them. The second critical step is to forgive your parents if they did something wrong—and all parents do to some degree. The third step is to submit this area of your life to the Lord. Acknowledging your failure and weakness, you must allow the Lord to give you strength and to teach you how to communicate in a righteous, healthy manner. There is nothing that cannot be forgiven, overcome, and changed with the Lord's help.

Four Important Foundations for Building an Atmosphere of Positive Communication

Once we understand how to identify destructive communication traits, we then need to understand the foundations of positive communication. Volumes have been written on the importance and techniques of proper communication. These four foundations are basic principles that are easy to understand and remember. They give us a good basis to begin to practice healthy communication. The four foundations are as follows:

1. The Foundation of a Positive Atmosphere

You'll never be able to talk in your family if the atmosphere is one of emotional darkness, negativity, and criticism. The Psalms tell us a powerful truth related to God. Psalm 100:4 says, *"Enter into His gates with thanksgiving, and into His courts with praise. Be thankful to Him, and bless His name."* According to this Scripture, the secret to entering God's presence is praise and thanksgiving. God's heart opens to the positive person who approaches Him. The book of Genesis tells us that God created us in His image. Therefore, all of us, whether we realize it or not, open our hearts to those who are positive, and close our hearts to those who are negative.

A person's spirit opens up when praised, but closes when criticized. Therefore, within the family, we need to be each other's cheerleaders. Husbands need to root for their wives, and wives for their husbands. Parents need to root for their kids. In fact, the parent should be more positive about his or her child than anyone that child will be around.

We all tend to gravitate toward those who affirm us. That is why the home needs to have a positive, affirming atmosphere. In a home with a positive atmosphere, the husband can't wait to get home because that is where he is affirmed and built up. He feels special. The wife can't wait to see her husband because she knows he is going to build her up and speak loving things to her. The children love to be with their parents because they are feeding them by speaking loving and positive things to them and about them.

The devil knows that if your home becomes a place of darkness or a place of poisoned words, you won't be able to relate to each other and open up to each other. That's why he does everything he can to take our mouths and turn them into swords that cut, wound, and kill. In such an atmosphere, no one opens his heart. The kids run to their friends and say more to them than they do to their parents. The wife turns to her friends or family; the husband turns to his friends or activities. The result is an emotionally barren home where everyone is closed and distant—all because of a negative spirit.

To build a positive atmosphere, we need to make praise a daily discipline—a fixture in our lives. Beginning with our relationship with the Lord, we need to praise Him daily. Psalm 118:24 says, *"This is the day the LORD has made; we will rejoice and be glad in it."* Praise is our decision. There is always something to be thankful for, and praise finds it. Every single day, we must be careful to make the decision to praise God. If we don't, not only will we forget the good things in our lives and the people around us, but we will also, without fail, begin to be negative and critical.

In addition to our discipline of praising and thanking God, we need to do the same for each other. We need to constantly remind our spouses, our children, and ourselves what is right with our families. As we praise the good things, a wonderful atmosphere of light and joy is built. We are endeared to each other because of the affirmation and encouragement that is shared. Also, when we praise, we earn the right to correct. I have heard it said many times that for every negative comment made, it takes seven positive comments to make up for it. Therefore, if our ratio of positive to negative comments isn't at least 7 to 1, we are building a negative atmosphere in our relationships.

Even when we complain or bring correction, we must be careful to do it in a positive way. We don't say to our children, "You little monster, why did you do that?" Instead, we say, "You are such a good child, and I love you so much. You have so much potential, and I want you to do better than this." Toward our spouses, we don't nitpick, complain, and insult; we lovingly speak the truth in an atmosphere of affirmation, commitment, and praise.

2. The Foundation of Fun and Humor

It's often overlooked in serious discussions of the qualities of a healthy family, but there needs to be humor in the home. God is merciful, so He almost always puts at least one comedian in each family. We need to be thankful for people who bring joy into our families and respect the benefit of their influence.

Humor should never be crude or at someone else's expense. Sarcasm is a dangerous form of humor because it is almost always rooted in anger. Therefore, sarcasm is most often a dishonest and indirect means of communicating something wrong. Humor in a home also needs to be pure. Dirty jokes or unclean humor is wrong for the obvious reasons.

Humor also shouldn't replace or circumvent discussion when it is needed. When something bad has happened or someone in the family is suffering, we first of all need to let everyone involved know that we care about the situation and are committed to resolving it properly. It can be very emotionally damaging when you are hurting or are having a problem and the people around you are making fun of it. Humor should not be expressed until after every effort has been made to express concern and a commitment to help.

Even then, humor always needs to be sensitive to the emotions of others.

"Humor" means an ability to enjoy each other and to have a positive attitude about life. Many hurtful and negative situations can be dealt with much easier if we keep things in the right perspective. When a couple or family stops laughing and having fun together, an atmosphere can quickly develop where problems become looming monsters and difficulties become dead ends.

We need to plan times to enjoy each other and laugh—a family game night for playing cards or games together, a special outing to go someplace fun, short trips or extended vacations together, weekly dates for couples—all of these are ways a family retains a spirit of enjoyment and fun. Family relationships should be fun. We all enjoy being around people with a wholesome sense of humor. In our marriage and family relationships, we need to keep things in perspective and not let the pressures and problems of life rob us of our joy.

3. The Foundation of Safe and Open Sharing

A successful family is a safe place to share one's heart. There is a consistency of love and expression of sincere concern, making each person worthy of trust. The home should be a sanctuary where any member can come and open his or her heart.

Children need to know that they can share anything with their parents. When our son, Brent, was five years old, he asked me one evening during dinner the meaning of a vulgar word he'd heard a friend use. It was *the* word you don't want to hear your child use. Inwardly, I may have been shocked (Karen and Julie certainly were), but I kept my cool and told Brent, in matter-of-fact terms he could understand, that it was a word the devil made up to try to make a very beautiful thing look dirty. I gave him a very general definition of sex and told him that God created it as a beautiful expression of love between a husband and wife. He accepted my explanation, and that was that.

I want my children to come to me for answers, not to their friends. I don't want them to learn about sex on TV or from movies. God has entrusted the discipling of children into the hands of their parents. It isn't the responsibility of the church or school. Those are only extensions of the parents, not replacements for them.

In an open atmosphere, children will know and understand that they can talk about anything. That candor must exist between husband and wife as well. Early in our marriage, Karen would say things to me and I would say, "Karen, that's dumb. You're just an emotional female. You need to get a grasp on things." By saying hurtful things like that, I shamed her and forced her to withdraw from me. She didn't feel safe to share because of my insensitivity. Today, Karen knows that everything in her life is important to me, and I want her to be able to talk to me about it. We have an atmosphere of openness.

Dysfunctional families seldom allow such an atmosphere. Certain subjects are not allowed to be discussed, and if you bring them up, you'll pay a heavy price. A successful family's response is, "We'll deal with our anger, our pain, our questions, and our needs. You can express yourself and not be judged, attacked, or condemned."

An atmosphere of safe and open sharing also means getting rid of all the distractions that prohibit meaningful conversation. When someone says he or she needs to talk to you, put the newspaper down, turn off the TV, and give that person your undivided attention.

When he or she is finished speaking, be very careful with your response. What is said is very important. In many families, there is never an opportunity to talk. The average father in America spends little time in meaningful dialogue with his children daily. Many parents are too busy and stressed out. Not only do they not take the time to talk to their children, but they also don't have time to talk to each other. In this situation, the child and spouse begin to feel rejected and unimportant.

Children many times don't know how to communicate the pain in their lives. Abused children often show signals of abuse, but only someone who cares about that child will pick up on it, because it is underlying. Many times people are communicating something that they're not saying verbally. You will never pick up on it unless you are making eye contact and listening. If you really listen, you'll find out that they're hurting and wondering if anyone loves them. They may feel that they're not special or normal. They may be worried about something and just need to know that someone cares. An open atmosphere is one that communicates to your family that they are more special than TV, work, the newspaper, friends, or anything else. When people in your family know that you're listening and are approachable, you will be providing a safe place with a loving atmosphere, and the words will be able to flow.

4. The Foundation of Conflict Resolution

Every marriage and family will have conflicts to deal with. Dysfunctional families are always characterized by unresolved tension and problems. Because they don't deal with their problems, or they try to deal with them in the wrong way, their problems remain and constantly affect their ability to relate.

Successful families deal with their problems. The loving atmosphere in their homes isn't a facade to hide their problems; it is a genuine spirit that is present because problems are dealt with in a positive and successful manner. Here are some important principles to help you resolve conflicts in your marriage and family relationships:

Deal With Conflicts on a Daily Basis.

Ephesians 4:26–27 says,

> *"'Be angry, and do not sin': do not let the sun go down on your wrath, nor give place to the devil."*

There is nothing essentially wrong with anger. All of us will be angry many times in our lives. In fact, nothing is more certain to grate our emotions at times than a close relationship with a family member. Since we are going to experience anger and need to be honest about it, the real issue is how we deal with it.

The Scripture text in Ephesians, chapter 4, tells us to be honest about our anger, but not to sin. We need to express our anger when we feel it, but in a healthy way. We also need to express our anger today and not let it build up or accumulate. Ephesians 4:27 warns us that if we go to bed on our anger, we give a foothold to the devil. Yesterday's anger is one of the most destructive forces in a marriage and family.

Don't let issues accumulate, or you will give the devil an open door into your life to taint your emotions and to accuse the person you are angry toward. Some people who say they've fallen out of love with their spouses are in that condition because their suppressed, unresolved emotions have deadened them internally. Also, because of their unresolved feelings, Satan has had the opportunity to interpret their emotions and to try to convince them to give up on the relationship.

Even when people say they're "out of love," they're not. The positive emotions they once felt are simply being clouded over by unresolved tensions. Once issues are resolved in marriages and families, love and affection are quickly resurrected. However, unresolved anger and problems can create such a profound sense of emotional distress and deadness that often the result is divorce or major problems. This is why we must be so vigilant to deal with problems daily in our marriages and families.

When we are committed to dealing with our problems on a daily basis, we also need to understand how important it is to expose our emotions to the Lord daily. Sometimes it might be difficult or even impossible to get someone to work with us to resolve a conflict. In those times, we can still deal with our emotions and close the door on the devil by taking our anger and grief quickly to the Lord. Turning upward in those times brings peace and a divine perspective to our situation. Even when we are able to work things out with a person, prayer brings a quicker and more meaningful resolve.

Deal With Conflicts in a Positive Manner.

When we deal with our emotions while they are fresh, we are at a big advantage. As we begin to try to resolve our emotions with our spouses, children, or parents, it is often tempting to begin with threats or hostile words. One couple I counseled for marriage difficulties started every argument with one of them shouting, "I don't know if this marriage is worth it or not; I may just have to call my lawyer!"

One young man who was a rebellious drug addict came from a home where his mother regularly called him "stupid" rather than by his name. I guess she thought the negative name-calling would wake him up and change his behavior. She was wrong.

Every encounter with a family member should begin with affirmation. Spouses should begin conflict resolution by stating their love, admiration, and commitment to each other. This is a critical element in conflict resolution. If we know that we are loved, it is much easier to deal with problems. However, if someone approaches us with their guns blazing and an angry countenance, we become immediately defensive.

As I have stated earlier in this chapter, parents must never call their children names unless they are good ones. They must also affirm children before and after discipline. This positive reinforcement lets our children know that we love them in spite of what is taking place. It also trains them for resolving conflicts with their peers, future spouses, and families.

Confront in a Humble Manner.

When addressing an issue with a family member, is your number one goal to win or to resolve the problem? What if you *are* the problem? When a spirit of humility characterizes an approach to conflict resolution, the answer to the problem is easy to reach because one or both parties are willing to look objectively at both sides and take responsibility for their own actions. Their desire isn't to win; it's to redeem the relationship and to protect the emotions of the one they love.

Pride is one of the most deadly forces in a relationship. Pride doesn't want to make peace; it wants to rule. Pride isn't willing to accept fault; it demands others accept the blame for the sake of protecting one's dominant position.

Jesus washed the feet of the disciples and commanded that they follow His example. The spouse, parent, or family member who is ready for conflict resolution must crucify the pride in his or her life and be willing to be humble. True conflict resolution doesn't take place through domination, intimidation, or manipulation. It takes place as we humbly sit at each other's feet, willing to serve each other for the sake of the relationship.

Listen.

As parents, we need to listen to our children. Many times, the things they are saying may be wrong or immature, but they need to be heard. We also need to listen to what our children are telling us about ourselves. Even though it's hard to admit, sometimes we are wrong in how we deal with them, and we need to acknowledge it before it causes an offense in our children. Even though all children have a sin nature, there are some children who are more rebellious than others because of an offense against their parents that the parents were unwilling to acknowledge or deal with.

I know a couple who are absolutely unwilling to admit that they ever made a mistake with their children. Any time one of their children says their mom or dad hurt them in some way or made a mistake in raising them, the parents become hostile and declare the child is the problem—never them!

If we are so threatened that we will not sit down with someone and listen to their grievances about us, there is something wrong with us.

Are we willing to listen to our children when they say we're being unfair? Maybe their criticism is true. If I listen to it and weigh it carefully, I grow as a man, as a parent, as a human being, and I become more sensitive to the hearts of others.

I believe every man needs to ask his wife what she sees wrong in him and what she'd like to see him change about himself. Most women I've met are fair, very relational, and highly intuitive. Most of what they have to say is valuable and needs to be said. More importantly, it needs to be heard and *listened to* by the husband! When we are willing to listen to the voices and hearts of our family members, we can deal with the issues that would otherwise tear us apart. Not to listen is to build resentment.

Wives also need to listen to their husbands. As a husband expresses his needs, hurts, fears, and frustrations, a truly listening wife can register what is being said and meet it with a sensitive, timely response.

One of the reasons conflicts are never resolved in families is that the members simply will not listen to each other. We would all do well to heed the admonition of James 1:19, *"So then, my beloved brethren, let every man be swift to hear, slow to speak, slow to wrath."*

Resolve the Issue.

As you deal with issues in a marriage and family, it is very important to bring them to a conclusion and resolve. Sometimes this is done by arriving at an agreement. As we end a conversation, it is important that we don't finish by stomping off or by making a negative comment like, "Well, I hope you'll remember next time this happens not to make the same mistake!" We need to end conversations with kindness and resolve.

Sometimes it helps to restate the final resolve of a situation until both parties agree. If there has been a mistake made, it is also important to repent to each other and to forgive. Repentance is important because it lets the other person know that we are accepting responsibility for our actions and that we take them seriously. Forgiveness is critical because it brings the issue to a resolve. True forgiveness means "I won't take this out on you in the future or bring it up again in a negative way."

When resolving issues with our children, it is also important to bring it to a resolve. When spanking or other forms of discipline are finished, we need to let our children know that they are loved and forgiven. We shouldn't let children grow up in an atmosphere of disapproval or emotional disfavor.

I believe the greatest way of all to bring issues to a final resolve is through prayer. I have never counseled a couple for serious marriage problems who pray together regularly. I have also never counseled a couple for serious problems who resolve their conflicts daily.

Praying together creates a bond between us that is greater than us. It invites God into the situation to heal hurt feelings, to give us strength to change, and to reignite our passions. The old saying "The family that prays together, stays together" is true.

Positive communication and conflict resolution are learned skills all of us can master. Understanding how critically important communication is in a marriage and how desperately the devil wants to attack us in this area, we need to commit ourselves every day to a life of growing and learning how to communicate better. The benefits are well worth the effort. Begin to challenge yourself today to practice healthy, positive communication and conflict resolution. Your marriage and family will never be the same!

SECRET FIVE

Proper Parental Authority

A healthy family is characterized by order and mutual respect. These elements are present in families where proper parental authority is exercised. God has invested in parents an authority that flows from Him for the purpose of extending His will into their families and beyond. This truth is illustrated in Matthew, chapter 6. In this text, Jesus taught us to pray what is commonly called "The Lord's Prayer." In this prayer, we are instructed to pray daily,

"Your kingdom come. Your will be done on earth as it is in heaven"
Matthew 6:10

The word "kingdom" means "direct rule and authority." Therefore, our daily prayer should include an appeal to God for an extension of His authority and will into our personal lives, marriages, families, and extending into every other area of our lives.

The focus of the submitted Christian life is to submit to the authority and will of God every day. In this way, we live in the blessing of God's peace and presence. The Bible teaches us that authority is from God and is for our good (Romans 13). Submission to authority is considered a virtue, and rebellion is serious sin (I Samuel 15:22–23). Therefore, parental authority is a necessary, righteous influence that promotes God's will and prevents our sin nature from destroying the potential of each individual family member and the family as a whole.

Another important point that needs to be made about parental authority is the importance the Bible puts on children obeying and honoring their parents. One of the most powerful promises in the Bible is connected to the commandment for us to honor our mothers and fathers.

> *Children, obey your parents in the Lord, for this is right. "Honor your father and mother," which is the first commandment with promise: "that it may be well with you and you may live long on the earth."* Ephesians 6:1–3

The Bible commands a child to obey and honor his or her parents. This is the first of the Ten Commandments God gave Moses that carried such a profound promise. God is trying to communicate something to us concerning the values of His kingdom as well as the importance of authority and submission. Therefore, the parents who do not exercise righteous authority and require their children to obey and honor them aren't only creating problems for themselves and society; they are also cursing their children with a life of problems, separated from the blessings and promises of God.

Even though everything you just read about authority is true, it is the opposite of what the world around us says. In our present world, submission is thought to be a sign of a weak mind, and rebellion is considered an attribute to be respected. Just look around at the movie stars making the most money, the athletes getting the most attention, and the people being celebrated most in our nation; you will soon find that few, if any of them, are committed, submitted Christians. The truth is, most of them are godless egomaniacs with a rebel spirit.

The children of America are being bombarded with messages of rebellion from television, movies, music, and peers. Wives are belittled if they respect and honor their husbands. Men are persecuted if they try to be godly, faithful husbands and fathers. To prove this point, the secular media, homosexuals, and radical women's groups have verbally attacked the national Promise Keepers movement among men. This proves how far our nation has fallen.

In order for us to begin to stop the wholesale destruction of the marriages and families in America and to build solid foundations for family life, we must totally reject the rebellious message of the world around us and begin to pray for God's righteous authority in our homes. As we do this, we must unapologetically begin to exercise righteous parental authority. It is an essential element for domestic success and survival. When proper parental authority is present, it creates the framework for lasting, loving relationships. When it is absent, it invites the most horrible influences from within and without to destroy one's marriage and family.

To help us build an understanding of the elements necessary for the establishing and maintaining of proper authority, the remainder of this chapter will be used to explain the three traits of proper parental authority.

Three Traits of Proper Parental Authority

1. Proper parental authority demonstrates submission to authority.

I often tell people that parenting is more caught than taught. What your children see in you is a more powerful influence than what you say to them and tell them to do. Consequently, when parents have a strand of rebellion coursing through their own personalities, they are bound to raise the level of rebellion that naturally exists in their children. These parents will have a more difficult time keeping their children's rebellion under control because their lives are contradictions of their demands upon their children.

The Apostle Paul had a message for the fathers in the church at Ephesus:

"And you, fathers, do not provoke your children to wrath, but bring them up in the training and admonition of the Lord"
Ephesians 6:4

Paul exhorts fathers not to provoke their children to wrath. The primary way fathers do this is by requiring something of their children that they are unwilling to do themselves. When parents are hypocritical and refuse to live by the same standards they impose on their children, it causes immediate resentment on the part of the children as well as the rejection of parental standards.

After Paul tells fathers not to provoke their children, he then commands them to bring their children up in the *"training ... of the Lord."* Training a child is different from telling or verbally instructing. To train a child means to model for a child what is desired for him to do. As a living example, reveal to him the proper way to love God, love others, and encounter life. In this way, children learn through verbal and visual messages they can accept.

In understanding the importance of this issue, husbands, wives, and parents need to think about their attitudes concerning authority and what they are communicating to their children. Our real disposition toward submission to authority can be revealed by honest answers to some of these questions:

- Am I really submitted to God's authority? Do I pray before I make decisions and consult the Word of God for answers?
- Do I believe authority is necessary for my life? Do I see God's authority, the authority of my pastor, my boss, and my spouse as needed and positive influences in my life, or as negative influences to restrain my need for expression and pleasure?
- Am I correctable? Do I have a teachable spirit? What is my response when I am confronted or corrected by authority?
- Do I speak negatively of police, government leaders, church leaders, my boss at work, or other leaders?

- Do I demonstrate the attitude toward the authorities in my life that I want from my children? If my children grow up to be like me, will God bless them?
- Do I reinforce the authority figures who are trying to keep my child in account (teachers, etc.), or do I take up my child's offense against them and dispute their authority?

Honest answers to these questions will help us to see if we meet the first condition for proper parental authority. As we examine our hearts concerning these issues, we must realize that our children's lives, both present and future, will be profoundly influenced by their attitudes toward authority. The parents who model and exercise proper authority in their children's lives are doing something incredibly important for their children and for themselves.

Be a good example to your children by displaying a positive attitude toward authority. Also, at times when you disagree with an authority figure or maybe even the government, let your children see you praying for them and making a righteous appeal. Train your children in how to deal with offenses and differences toward authority in a righteous manner. At times when an authority figure may be in sin or pressuring your child to sin, teach your child how to refuse sinful behavior without demonstrating a spirit of rebellion. Old Testament figures such as Daniel, Joseph, and Esther are wonderful role models of how to live an uncompromising life under unrighteous authority. Teach your children these Bible stories and talk to them about how we are to respond to authority, whether it is righteous or unrighteous.

2. Proper parental authority honors God's order for men and women.

I was once counseling a couple for marriage problems who had a reversed-role marriage. The husband was passive and compliant, and his wife was aggressive and dominant. This is a common scenario in many marriages. Of course, it never works. The husband, regardless of how good-natured he may seem, feels emasculated by his wife and resents her dominance. The wife, though strong, resents and disrespects the weakness in her husband.

As I was counseling this couple for their problems, they began to tell me about the behavior of their children. This couple had one son and two daughters. The boy, who was twelve years old, was demonstrating extreme aggression and resentment toward his sisters and his mother. The daughters, fourteen and nine, were both demonstrating troubling signs of dominance and resentment toward men.

Even though every child has immature attitudes at times regarding the opposite sex, the child who grows up in a home where sexual roles are reversed or are not clearly defined is at a disadvantage. After this couple told me about their children and their behavior toward the opposite sex, I communicated to them that their children were simply responding to the environment of their home. That caught them completely off guard. They had never connected their marriage relationship and behavior toward one another with the behavior of their children.

As odd as it seems, many parents don't realize the fact that everything they do is communicating something to their children about their own sex and the opposite sex. As a man relates to his wife, he is communicating to his daughters how to view men—good or bad. He is modeling to them what to expect from men and marriage. He is also training his sons in how to treat women and to be treated by them.

As a woman relates to her husband, she is training her sons how to view women and how to relate to them. She is also training her daughters how to treat men and to respond to them.

Our modeling of sex roles to our children is critical in their development. The couple who were having problems with their son being resentful and their daughters being dominant and aggressive are good examples. The son had built a resentment toward his sisters and mother for their dominant behavior. Even though his father was willing to put up with it, his son had the opposite reaction. This is what happens when sex roles are reversed.

Your children will either follow your example or reject it totally. Either way, they have been misled by your example. Many men who dominate women today were either raised in homes where their fathers did the same to their mothers, or they were raised in homes with weak fathers and dominant mothers; they swore that a woman would never dominate them again. The same principle applies to many dominant females.

The couple's two young daughters who were showing aggression toward their brother, father, and men in general had simply learned from their mother how to treat men. The father's passive behavior and the brother's aggressive behavior simply reinforced in the daughters' own minds their need to mistrust and dominate men. Innocently, these two girls were being set up for a life of frustration and pain because of the mismodeling of sex roles they were witnessing in their parents' lives.

Proper parental authority must be built upon a proper relationship between a couple and God as well as between each other. For a single parent, this would mean that you must be true to your own gender role, regardless of the extra responsibilities you may have to assume.

Regardless of your personality or how you have been raised, your sex role should never be dictated by your past or any other cultural influence. Your sex role in marriage must be based upon the Word of God and God's design for your life. Any other standard is insufficient and will not provide the foundation for personal fulfillment, success in marriage, or proper role modeling to your children.

The perfect marriage related to every category of success is described in Ephesians, chapter 5. I'm sure you have read this text before, but I want you to read it again carefully and see what it says about the sex roles and responsibilities of a righteous man and woman.

Wives, submit to your own husbands, as to the Lord.
For the husband is head of the wife, as also Christ is head of the
church; and He is the Savior of the body.

Therefore, just as the church is subject to Christ, so let the wives be to their own husbands in everything.
Husbands, love your wives, just as Christ also loved the church and gave Himself for her, that He might sanctify and cleanse her with the washing of water by the word, that He might present her to Himself a glorious church, not having spot or wrinkle or any such thing, but that she should be holy and without blemish.
So husbands ought to love their own wives as their own bodies; he who loves his wife loves himself.
For no one ever hated his own flesh, but nourishes and cherishes it, just as the Lord does the church.
For we are members of His body, of His flesh and of His bones.
"For this reason a man shall leave his father and mother and be joined to his wife, and the two shall become one flesh."
This is a great mystery, but I speak concerning Christ and the church. Nevertheless let each one of you in particular so love his own wife as himself, and let the wife see that she respects her husband.
Ephesians 5:22–33

This passage describes the perfect marriage. An honoring female is married to a sacrificial male. He is strong, but he uses his strength to exalt and honor his wife. She is his equal, but she uses the sacrificial love he gives her to love him and honor him. This couple is deeply in love, and their behavior perpetuates their affection and meets the deep needs in each other.

Even though we might not have this type of marriage today, the Christian couple needs to make this their desire—their goal. Doing so creates an accountability to a true standard. When a husband is selfish and abusive, he knows he is wrong because he has violated the pattern of the Word of God. When a wife is dishonoring and dominant, she knows that she has transgressed Biblical standards. When they both have the right standard and stay accountable to it, they begin to make progress toward order and mutual respect in their home.

The reason this point is so important isn't just because of our sex-role modeling for our children; it is also because we can't produce something in our children that isn't in us. We can't give away something that we don't have. The reason many couples can't produce order and respect in their children is because there is none in their own relationship. The disorder and rebellion in their children is a projection of their own relationship. It is illogical to expect children to attain to a higher level than their parents.

There is a story in the fourth chapter of Mark's Gospel about a time when Jesus spoke to the sea and said, *"Peace, be still!"* (Mark 4:39). The disciples and Jesus were caught in a terrible storm. The disciples were afraid that their boat was about to capsize and they were going to drown. However, as soon as Jesus said, *"Peace, be still!"* everything around them became peaceful. The reason Jesus could produce peace externally is because He was filled with it internally. The reason the disciples were powerless over the storm was because they were filled with fear and anxiety. The storm around them was a mirror of their own souls.

Moms and dads, you just can't produce in your children something you don't have. If your home is filled with chaos and confusion, don't blame the kids; examine your own heart and relationship. As soon as you begin to deal with your relationship with God and your spouse and become obedient to what God's Word says, you will find a new and natural authority that will extend to your children as well.

Proper parental authority isn't a dominant position of demanding rules and harsh discipline; it is a living example of Biblical submission to God's order for our lives. As we reveal to our children this order, not only do we endow them with a true image of sex roles and a model of genuine success, but we are also empowered with a God-given authority. The order and respect within us can calm the seas of our family life with a simple command. Because it is in us, it can now flow naturally and powerfully from us.

3. Proper parental authority enforces loving, consistent discipline.

It would be wonderful if our children didn't have a sin nature and were naturally good. This is what secular humanism teaches. Almost all of the teaching related to parenting and child discipline that is being taught in our schools, universities, magazines, and in the media is based upon the belief that children are naturally good and that their problems stem from domestic and societal dysfunction. Therefore, according to secular humanistic teaching, discipline for a child is cruel and counterproductive. According to humanistic belief, all children need is patient redirection in order to be put in touch with their "natural goodness."

As I said earlier, it would be nice if our children were naturally obedient and sinless. However, it's not true. Not only are we told in the Bible that we all have a sin nature (Isaiah 53:6 / Romans 3:23), but reality also reveals the fact that children are inherently selfish, rebellious, and foolish. Those three factors are a dangerous combination. It is amazing to me that secular humanists can believe as they do. Do these people have kids?

Of course, even with their imperfections, we love our children; they are wonderful gifts from God. Our job as parents is to be good stewards of them as we protect, nurture, and train them for success. We don't measure success primarily in monetary terms or according to the standards of society. Proper parental authority measures success by the development of godly character and eternal values. Therefore, a Biblical view of our children and God's standards for their character and development is essential.

As we begin to raise our children, we will notice very early in their lives the first glimpses of a rebellious spirit. As soon as they are able to understand simple commands, we need to start by clearly and lovingly communicating to them what we expect for them to do; then we need to make sure they understand.

The first time I disciplined my daughter, Julie, she was a little over one year old. We were at my grandmother's house, and she was about to grab a china cup. I walked over to where she was and told her, "No, no, don't touch the cup." I gently picked her up and moved her across the room where she had been playing earlier.

It didn't take her thirty-seconds to get back across the room to that cup. As she started reaching for it again, she looked at me over her shoulder with a guilty look. I smiled at her and said, "No, no. Don't touch or Daddy will spank your hand." I swatted my own hand to show her what would happen if she touched it. She smiled back at me and grabbed the cup. I walked across the room and gently swatted her hand, again saying, "No, no. Don't touch the cup."

Julie cried when I spanked her hand. I picked her up and comforted her, told her I loved her and made sure she understood everything was all right. As soon as she was settled, I put her back down and told her to play, but not to touch the cup. She had fun and didn't touch it again.

My children are both grown. In raising them, I never scarred them, abused them, or had to go to extremes to keep them under control. The reason was because from the time they began to express rebellion, Karen and I lovingly and consistently disciplined them. In doing so, we were able to enjoy our children to the fullest, and they were able to live in a safe, productive atmosphere.

We still have a great relationship with our children, and they have turned out to be well-adjusted, successful young adults. Karen and I are so proud of them, and we think that we have the greatest kids in the world. (Of course, we are very prejudiced!)

It is a pitiful thing to watch parents begging their children to behave or trying to manage rebellion without exercising true authority. With the misinformation about parenting from secular humanists and the erosion of authority in America today, it is easy for parents to feel confused and helpless. Even though it's common, it's wrong. Regardless of whether the government, modern psychology, or the media agrees or not, parents are endowed with authority by God; they need to use it for the sake of their children and our society.

The "experts" in America are constantly changing their minds about what is right and wrong, good and bad, acceptable and unacceptable. Their counsel is like shifting sand. Every decade the rules change. If you raise your children according to their advice, you can waste your energies, only to find out that what you did for them is now found to be wrong—and now they've discovered "a better way."

I want to remind you that God has the best way. His standards are eternal and will never change. Therefore, when you trust in what God's Word says and raise your children accordingly, you will succeed. To help you understand some basic principles in how to properly discipline your children, here are some guidelines to follow:

Four Guidelines for Effective Discipline

1. Clearly communicate your expectations and the penalty for violation.

Effective parenting begins by patiently explaining to your children the difference between right and wrong. As parents, we need to talk to our children, instruct them, and build such a relationship with them that we can explain to them our expectations fully and kindly. It is improper to bark commands at children or discipline them for something they don't understand. Children will grow up resentful and insecure if they are not informed patiently and fully.

As you tell your children what you expect for them to do and not do, tell them what will happen if they violate certain rules. Of course, the punishment should be fair. Use common sense. If you are too strict, you will harm your children and crush their spirits. If you are too lenient, you won't get their attention or be able to restrain their behavior.

In 1995, I interviewed Gary Smalley for our television program. Gary is a well-known speaker, author, and expert on marriage and family relationships. In speaking of his own family, he told about how they developed a "family constitution" that hangs on the wall of their home. Gary got the idea from a law enforcement official who had a great deal of experience with delinquent children and teens.

Gary, his wife, and children discussed together the rules of the home and the punishment for breaking each rule. As they adopted the rules, they wrote them down on paper. When they were finished, they mounted them and hung them on the wall for everyone to see.

This is a great way to make sure everyone understands the rules and the punishment for breaking them.

One of the greatest needs among children today is for clearly defined rules. Because of the absence and apostasy of many parents today, kids don't have clearly defined rules to live by. This creates confusion and frustration in children. It also causes them to be much more susceptible to peer pressure because they are having to find their own way. Clear, fair standards that are communicated to children in patient, loving terms lay the groundwork for effective discipline.

2. Be consistent in discipline.

When you tell your children something you expect of them and the penalty for violation, you must enforce discipline every time they transgress. If you do, you will teach your children that you mean what you say. Therefore, it will be much easier to keep them in control. If you don't, you will confuse them.

When you don't follow through on discipline, you are training your children not to listen to you. If you wait until you are finally so frustrated that you discipline them in anger, you are confusing them and causing resentment in them. One of the most dangerous problems of not disciplining children consistently is that your emotions can get out of control. This is where the majority of child abuse comes from. For the sake of the parents and the child, both parents in the home must consistently enforce standards of conduct.

Another serious problem about inconsistency is that it misleads a child concerning God. As parents, we must realize that we are the greatest influence in forming our children's concept of God. When parents don't follow through on discipline, they are teaching their children that God doesn't mean what He says. That is incorrect. When God gives a promise or a warning to us, He follows through one hundred percent of the time. If we are going to properly parent our children and reflect God's nature correctly, we must also follow through.

3. Discipline in love.

When you have communicated your expectations and your child

has misbehaved, it is then time to enforce your standards. In doing so, it is up to the parent to decide which method of punishment is most appropriate and effective. We must remember that discipline is something we do *for* our children, not just *to* them. It isn't designed to give us emotional satisfaction or to satisfy our need for revenge; it is meant to build within our children a respect for authority and to create a mental connection between disobedience and displeasure.

As we consider how to discipline, here are our options:

Spanking—Swatting on the bottom with a paddle or wooden instrument (not beating or flailing and not with your hand). Even though it is highly controversial in our society, it is the most recommended form of discipline in the Bible (Proverbs 13:24; 22:15; 23:13–14; 29:15). Proper spanking is good because it is swift, effective, and it is over. It doesn't linger for hours or days. It deals with the problem promptly and is finished. However, even though it is effective, it is still not the answer for every situation.

Grounding—Restriction from certain friends, activities, or pleasures. For smaller children, this can also be called a timeout. For older adolescents and teens, grounding can last for anywhere from a day to many weeks. For a young child, it should be much shorter—normally anywhere from ten minutes to a few hours. This would involve restriction from toys, friends, television, etc.

Extra chores—Taking out the trash, cleaning, working in the yard, etc.

Restitution and repentance—Addressing a person or a situation the child has violated by acknowledgment of guilt, asking for forgiveness, and restoring anything that was damaged or taken. This type of discipline is especially appropriate when a child has abused another child (brother, sister, friend) or has committed an offense against society.

As soon as we have chosen our method of discipline, we need to be careful how we administer it. If we are consistent in our discipline, our emotions shouldn't be out of control. If we aren't in control of our emotions, we should take a few minutes to cool down before administering the discipline. Once we are in control, we should try to speak to the child and correct him or her in a private place—not in front of his or her friends. Of course, children will hear us correct their brothers and sisters, but we must be careful not to scream at our children or shame them publicly.

The ideal situation for discipline is to remove the children to a private area. This is where we can explain to them that they have disobeyed and are going to be disciplined. We must not yell at them, call them names, or try to shame them. In a controlled voice, we must affirm them and our love for them. We need to tell them that we love them and are proud of them, but won't allow them to misbehave.

In a controlled, private area, communicate the discipline to the child if it is something other than spanking. If it is spanking, in the same private, loving environment, explain to the child that he or she has violated the rules and is going to be spanked. Many times a child will be bargaining, arguing, blaming, and crying by this time. In a kind but authoritative manner, a parent should have the child bend over the bed or a chair, and then the parent should administer two or three swats. The swats should be hard enough to hurt, but not hard enough to cause damage. A child should not be repeatedly swatted or swatted where it leaves bruises or permanent scars.

Once children have been disciplined, take them in your lap or next to you and give them affection. (Karen and I always prayed with our children after we disciplined them, asking God to bless them.) After loving them, praying for them, and affirming them, tell them to go have fun, but not to violate your standards again.

When children are disciplined in a consistent, loving manner, they feel accepted and secure. Loving discipline also produces an environment of peace in the home between parents and children and between siblings. Proper parental authority is a protective influence that enforces the rules in a relational, patient, consistent manner.

4. Keep the faith.

One of the most important ingredients of proper parental authority is faith. Hebrews 11:1 tells us, *"Now faith is the substance of things hoped for, the evidence of things not seen."* In parenting, it is impossible to immediately produce righteousness in our children—it is a long process. Even though there are immediate benefits to proper discipline, our children are still immature and make mistakes.

Many parents I talk to, regardless of the age of their children, are discouraged. They have done everything they know to do, yet their children are still pushing the limits and acting like, well, children! We must understand that the best parenting in the world takes time to have its full effect.

The parent who measures success by immediate change will live on a roller coaster of emotions. In fact, measuring success by immediate results will sometimes discourage us so much that we will either take our frustrations out on our children and feel as though they are abnormal, or we will give up, feeling like we are abnormal and inadequate—or both.

Parenting requires faith. Faith looks beyond the moment and sees the future. Faith acts with the belief that if we obey God and do what is right, God will honor our obedience with "eventual reward." If all results were immediate, we wouldn't need faith. Faith is necessary because much of what we do is against what reality reveals, what our emotions are telling us, and what the devil has to say.

Proverbs 22:6 tells us:

"Train up a child in the way he should go, and when he is old he will not depart from it."

This Scripture doesn't promise immediate results for the righteous, faithful parent—it promises eventual results. I heard someone once say that you don't really see the full fruits of your parenting until your child turns thirty years old. Many times it doesn't take that long, and sometimes it might even take longer; but the promise of Proverbs 22:6 is that the faithful investment of a righteous parent is never in vain.

Satan loves to discourage parents by taking a mental snapshot of their children in their worst moments and rubbing it in the parents' noses. Remember, parents, Ephesians 6:16 tells us:

"above all, taking the shield of faith with which you will be able to quench all the fiery darts of the wicked one."

Faith is a powerful force that gives us hope through the trials of life, a positive destination even when we are walking through *"the valley of the shadow of death"* (Psalm 23:4), and confidence to continue a course of action even when we aren't seeing immediate results. Our faith is based upon God's faithfulness, truth, and power of His Word. Raise your children by faith!

Even in the troubling days in which we live, God's Word is still true. Proper parental authority within a home vanquishes the forces of darkness that would come to sow rebellion and disorder as it extends the authority and will of God to the family. Dysfunctional families are places of disorder, sex-role confusion, and/or abusive authority. Successful families are homes where parents who are submitted to God and each other raise their children in an environment of clearly communicated expectations, fair and consistent discipline, and lots and lots of love.

SECRET SIX

The Virtue of Personal Responsibility

The doctrine of personal responsibility is one of the most basic truths in Scripture. It is founded upon the premise that we have been created in the image of God as free moral agents. God created us with a free will. In fact, everything we do is of our own choosing. Along with the freedom of choice God has given us, He has also given us the responsibility to use that freedom properly.

Perhaps the clearest Scripture in the entire Bible where this truth is expressed is in Deuteronomy 30:19. Speaking to Moses, God said,

> *"I call heaven and earth as witnesses today against you, that I have set before you life and death, blessing and cursing; therefore choose life, that both you and your descendants may live."*

In effect, God was saying to Moses and the children of Israel, "You're going into the Promised Land, and I set before you the opportunity for life or death, the opportunity to be blessed or cursed. Your destiny and that of your children is your responsibility. I have given you every opportunity for success; you are now responsible to make the correct decisions and obey what I have told you."

Obviously, the human race has encountered some serious problems with the issue of taking the responsibility to make the right choices. The problems didn't start with Moses and the children of Israel; they began in the Garden of Eden. The first dysfunctional family on earth was Adam and Eve and their children. Their story is a vivid portrayal of the importance of the issue of personal responsibility and the consequences for irresponsibility toward God and others.

In helping us to understand the concept of personal responsibility and how it affects our personal lives and families, we will look at five scenes from the lives of the first family on earth. Observing their fall and subsequent failures is both sobering and enlightening. It also underscores the extreme importance of the issue of personal responsibility and our need to honor it and teach it to our children.

SCENE ONE: The Seduction of Eve

Now the serpent was more cunning than any beast of the field which the LORD God had made. And he said to the woman, "Has God indeed said, 'You shall not eat of every tree of the garden'?"
And the woman said to the serpent, "We may eat the fruit of the trees of the garden; but of the fruit of the tree which is in the midst of the garden, God has said, 'You shall not eat it, nor shall you touch it, lest you die.'"
Then the serpent said to the woman, "You will not surely die. For God knows that in the day you eat of it your eyes will be opened, and you will be like God, knowing good and evil."
Genesis 3:1–5

As Satan entered the Garden of Eden, the first thing he tried to do was to convince Eve that God did not have her best interest in mind, and because of that, she had no responsibility to obey Him. That was the world's first lie, and it's still being pushed on us by the devil.

However, Scripture spells out clearly that our first responsibility in life is to honor and obey God.

We must remember that God created us. We are not simply the product of genetics; we are the product of the hand of God. Psalm 139:13–14 says:

> *"For You formed my inward parts; You covered me in my mother's womb. I will praise You, for I am fearfully and wonderfully made; marvelous are Your works, and that my soul knows very well."*

Because God created us, He has every right to tell us what to do and to set parameters on us. When we forget this and think we have the right to do as we please, we are in the same deception that caused Adam and Eve to rebel against God in the Garden of Eden. We will also share in the same results.

America is obsessed with personal rights. Even though our freedoms in America are precious, they must be balanced by personal responsibility, beginning with our responsibility to God. However, on an increasing basis, we are rejecting any form of personal responsibility, as we demand even greater rights. The spirit of our age is even having a very powerful influence on many Christians.

I have heard Christian wives and husbands tell me as they were having affairs or divorcing their mates that they "have a right to be happy." Some of them have even tried to convince their mates, children, families, and me that God provided their partner for adultery because He "knew I was unhappy and my needs weren't getting met." That is sick! It's time we grow up, stop getting our theology from TV talk shows, and go back to the Bible for our information.

We have a total responsibility to do what God tells us to do regardless of the price we have to pay, the sacrifice required, or the persecution we must endure. I Corinthians 6:20 tells us,

"For you were bought at a price; therefore glorify God in your body and in your spirit, which are God's."

The price we were bought with is the blood of Jesus Christ. The next time we balk at obedience because of what it will cost us, we need to remember what it cost God to set us free from sin.

Because God created us and has redeemed us from sin, He has every right to tell us what to do. The wonderful thing is that what God tells us to do is good for us and will bless our lives. God loves us more than we love ourselves. If we will obey Him, the result will be lives of freedom, peace, and fullness of joy.

II Corinthians 5:10–11 says:

For we must all appear before the judgment seat of Christ, that each one may receive the things done in the body, according to what he has done, whether good or bad. Knowing, therefore, the terror of the Lord, we persuade men; but we are well known to God, and I also trust are well known in your consciences.

The Bible tells us to prepare for the day when we will stand before the throne of God in judgment. On that day, our obedience or disobedience will be revealed. It will also be proven that we are totally responsible to God for everything we say and do, and that we have no right to do anything apart from what He desires. The fifth chapter of John's Gospel tells us that Jesus never did anything in His ministry on earth without His heavenly Father's approval. The message is simple: to be a follower of Christ, to be a son or daughter of God, is to live a life of obedience.

Paul writes in II Corinthians 5:11, *"... I also trust (that we) are well known in your consciences."* The word "conscience" isn't a word we hear a lot about these days. However, a conscience toward God is the cement that holds a family together. When a family loses their conscience toward God, they lose everything. There is no longer any moral restraint to hold them together or to prevent antisocial behavior.

When a man doesn't have a conscience toward God, there is nothing to prohibit immoral behavior on his part, or to cause him to sacrifice for his wife and family, because he is only accountable to himself. When a woman has no conscience toward God, she will do what she pleases, when she pleases. She makes her own rules. Again, there is no accountability. There is nothing to restrain her behavior. When children have no conscience toward God, chaos and rebellion break out. Outer controls are insufficient because there is no inner sense of responsibility to restrain them.

One of the chief duties of parents is to instill in their children a conscience toward God. This issue is critical. Without a conscience toward God, we are left to ourselves with no moral compass. However, with a strong sense of conscience, we are restrained and are able to restrain our children and our society as a whole.

The men who framed the Constitution of the United States presupposed that America was a godly nation of people with a conscience toward God. President John Adams said, "Our Constitution was made only for a moral and religious people. It is wholly inadequate to the government of any other." If America does not have a conscience toward God, more than our families is in danger of falling apart. Void of conscience, society as a whole begins to unravel. Law becomes meaningless, and police are no longer able to restrain lawbreakers.

This is what we are witnessing today. Because we as a society are rejecting God's Word as the standard for behavior and have largely lost a conscience toward God, we can no longer restrain crime and antisocial behavior. As James Dobson said, "We are in a moral free fall." Literally, we can't build prisons fast enough or hire enough law enforcement personnel to restrain our society. Besides the criminal element, immorality, sexual perversion, rebellion, and bizarre behavior are spreading like cancer throughout every community in America. The reason? We have lost our sense of conscience.

As parents, we must begin developing a sense of conscience in our children at an early age. The primary way we do this is by teaching them the Word of God. From the time our children are young, we need to read them the Bible and explain it to them. We need to read to them stories about Jesus, Paul, Joseph, Daniel, Esther, and other Bible characters. As we do, we will illustrate for them the difference between good and evil and the authority of God. We will teach them that lying is wrong, stealing is wrong, rebellion is wrong, and that the Bible is true.

When we open God's Word in our homes, it comes into our children's lives and builds a bridge for the Holy Spirit to begin communicating to their hearts. The Holy Spirit begins to convict them of right and wrong and reveals God's presence to them, building a deeper, stronger relationship with our children, until one day they have accepted Christ for themselves. By reading God's Word to our children and living by God's Word, there will be a full transference of faith and conviction from us to them through the work of the Holy Spirit.

Another way we can build a conscience toward God in our families is by praying about what we do. This lets our children know that our lives are under God's authority. When they were growing up, my children would come home many times and try to sway Karen and me in our decisions, especially the ones related to them. They would say, "Everybody else is doing it!"

I repeatedly told my children that in spite of what anyone else did or didn't do, our decisions were based on God's Word and prayer. I was trying to train them to be sensitive to the fact that we owe allegiance to God above any person. I was also trying to teach them how to pray about the practical issues of their lives on a daily basis.

When Julie and Brent were ready to buy their first cars, we made it a real project. We read *Consumer Reports*, shopped thoroughly, and prayed about it. We told them what price range we could afford, and that limited their options. One of the things I told the kids was, "God has a car for you somewhere. The car He provides will be better than any you could provide for yourself, so we need to start praying about it right now."

Their attitude was, "Well, you know, Dad, we think we kinda know what we want." I told them we are obligated to pray, and that

God is good; He'll be faithful to answer. So we prayed and waited for God's direction. Julie and Brent were both delighted with the cars they got, and both cars performed well mechanically.

As we pray and walk through the doors God opens for us, we will be in His perfect will, making good choices, being obedient, and being blessed with a rich, abundant life.

> *"... I set before you life and death, blessing and cursing ..."*
> Deuteronomy 30:19

How do we get the life and blessing? We do what Jesus says, because He is the Way, the Truth, and the Life. If we look to Him for guidance in our decision making, He will never lead us to a place of death or cursing.

SCENE TWO: The Silence of Adam

As the serpent seduced Eve and pursuaded her to rebel against God, Adam was silent. He was obviously present because Eve took the fruit and then turned and gave it to him. Adam had been watching the interchange going on between his wife and the serpent, but he hadn't said a word. Let me show you where the major problem was in Adam's behavior.

In the beginning, when God created Adam and Eve, the Bible says,

> *"Then God blessed them, and God said to them, 'Be fruitful and multiply; fill the earth and subdue it; have dominion over the fish of the sea, over the birds of the air, and over every living thing that moves on the earth'"*
> Genesis 1:28

When God created Adam and Eve, He commanded them to multiply and subdue the earth. The word "subdue" means "to bring into subjection by force." God's command to Adam and Eve was to take dominion over the earth, to go throughout the earth and bring everything under their rule. God gave them the authority and commanded them to use it.

Adam was irresponsible as he watched the serpent deceiving his wife. All he had to do, when he saw the serpent trying to seduce Eve, was to intervene or walk over and say, "Pardon me, Eve; I need to kill a snake." After killing it, he could have turned to Eve and said, "Now, honey, I don't think that was a good conversation, do you?" All he had to do was take authority and act. But Adam didn't do a thing. He just stood there—silent.

The devastation in most of the homes in our nation is the result of silent husbands, wives, and parents. Rather than standing up to the forces that are wreaking havoc in their homes and neighborhoods, many are casually observing as Satan destroys an entire generation. Like Adam, they are irresponsible in their duty to resist and "subdue" the forces of darkness seeking to destroy them and their children.

We have been given authority by God. It isn't just a blessing or gift; it is a responsibility. Speaking to His church, Jesus says,

"And I give you the keys of the kingdom of heaven, and whatever
you bind on earth will be bound in heaven, and whatever you loose
on earth will be loosed in heaven"
Matthew 16:19

Moms and dads, you can bind the evil in your home. You can kick the devil out the front door, or you can let him in; it's totally in *your* power, not his. You have the authority to rule your home righteously, whether you realize it or not.

By the same token, I fully believe the Church has the power to take authority over evil forces over our cities. I don't believe mayors, city commissioners, or police have the greatest authority in our cities; I believe the Church does. I believe that because Jesus told us whatever we bind on earth will be bound in heaven, and whatever we loose on earth will be loosed in heaven (Matthew 16:19).

Paul tells us in Ephesians, chapter 6 that we are not wrestling "against flesh and blood." In the big picture, the problems in our cities are not the things that people are doing. The Apostle Paul instructs us that our real battle is against "principalities and powers" in the heavenly places.

The Church is the only entity in a city that can do something about evil powers in the heavenlies that are seeking to destroy us. As God's Church, we have been given the authority to come against those powers, to subdue them, and to take dominion and authority over them in Jesus' name. The only question is—will we do it, or will we just stand back and say nothing?

Years ago, my hometown in Texas was in serious social and economic trouble. Bumper stickers all over town read, "Would the last person leaving Amarillo please turn out the lights?" There were other problems, including disunity and divisiveness among the churches, but the most pressing problems seemed to be economic.

During that time, about one hundred members of our congregation met weekly to pray. We cried out, "Father in heaven, we bind a spirit of division and discouragement in our city in the name of Jesus. Give us favor with businesses and in boardrooms across America. Make our city attractive to them so they will move their businesses from wherever they are across the United States to Amarillo. Bless our city leaders with wisdom and favor. Strengthen and protect our police officers. Bless the churches of our city, and bond our hearts together in love. Let this be a place of righteousness, unity, and prosperity." We prayed that prayer over and over and over.

Now, everything we prayed for has happened. Even though the city isn't perfect, it is dramatically different. As of the past few years and even now as I write this book, Amarillo has a great city government and police department, a growing and prosperous economy, and a wonderful unity among the pastors and churches. I praise God for His faithfulness!

We took authority! We stood up and said, "We won't take this! We won't live in this environment! We declare victory in the Name of Jesus!" Each and every one of us has the ability to rule if we will only stand up and exercise our authority to do so. Authority is not a religious toy; it's a responsibility. We have the responsibility to rule righteously and authoritatively. Joshua stood up and said,

"But as for me and my house, we will serve the Lord"
Joshua 24:15

As a mighty leader, Joshua declared with authority what he was going to do. He wasn't a man who was tossed around by the social tide; he was a man who reversed the tide by strong, decisive leadership.

Sometimes I compare Christianity to other religions when I think about the ideas of authority and rule. Take Islam, for example. Islam is the fastest growing religion in the world today. Muslims believe it is their responsibility in the name of Allah to bring this planet into submission. They believe that with all of their hearts and are aggressively building mosques all over the world. When I was in South Africa, they were building a mosque every fifty square miles. They are actively evangelizing with zeal and confidence.

What has happened to the real Church of Jesus Christ? Have we become so apathetic in our faith that we've become just like Adam? Why are our homes and communities being ravaged by sin and moral decay? It is because we will not use our God-given authority. As husbands, wives, and parents, we must realize that God holds us responsible for the condition of our homes and nothing, except God, has power over us without our permission—NOTHING!

Jesus said in Matthew 16:18, *"... I will build My church, and the gates of Hades shall not prevail against it."* Did you hear that? Jesus said the powers of hell wouldn't be able to withstand us or overcome us. He said this with the understanding that He had endowed us with incredible power. We need to rejoice in the fact that we have the authority to reverse and overcome the influence of sin and Satan in our marriages and families. Using the authority God has given us, we can live in freedom and success. However, if we don't use it, we're going to get nailed by the devil. Just like Adam, it won't happen because God isn't around or because we are victims; it will happen because we won't stand up and "subdue" the enemy.

We *have* the authority, but we need to act on that authority, stand up for what we believe, and take action. Here is a powerful Old Testament verse that underscores this truth:

"If My people who are called by My name will humble themselves,
and pray and seek My face, and turn from their wicked ways, then
I will hear from heaven, and will forgive their sin and heal
their land"
II Chronicles 7:14

God didn't give this incredible promise to the ACLU, the PTA, or a civic club. He said it about His people. If *you* will act, *I* will act. If *you* will use *your* authority, *I* will use *My* authority.

If you want it bound, bind it! If you want it loosed, loose it in the Name of Jesus. But, if you won't take action, the devil will. He's already working hard to get at your children. He is coming at them from a hundred angles to capture their souls. He also wants your marriage, your city, and your church. The one who is going to get all of these things is the one who wants them the most—the one who aggressively acts with the greater authority. Understand, *you* have greater authority! Use it!

We need to teach our children to use the authority they have through Jesus by teaching them a Biblical worldview. They need to know that there are good and evil forces. They also need to understand that we don't have to fear evil forces, but we must respect their potential for deception and destruction. As issues come up in our children's lives, we certainly don't want them to be spiritual "power mongers" or to be paranoid about a demon being behind every bush.

However, we do need to teach our children that people aren't always the issue. Spiritual forces over which we need to take authority control many issues in life. This is the text of Paul's writings in Ephesians, chapter 6, concerning spiritual warfare. He was addressing Christians who were faced with daily oppression, temptation, and attacks. There has never been a society more spiritually attacked than our own. Therefore, we and our children need to learn to put on the full armor of God daily as we take authority over the enemy.

SCENE THREE: The Shifting of the Blame

Genesis, chapter 3, records the sin of Adam and Eve. After they sinned, God confronted Adam and Eve concerning their sin. Here is the account of that conversation:

> *"... Have you eaten from the tree of which I commanded you that*
> *you should not eat?"*
> *Then the man said, "The woman whom You gave to be with me,*
> *she gave me of the tree, and I ate."*
> *And the LORD God said to the woman, "What is this you have*
> *done?" The woman said, "The serpent deceived me, and I ate."*
> Genesis 3:11–13

As God confronted Adam and Eve to hold them responsible for their behavior, they did something that is common for man—they transferred the blame. Adam blamed Eve. Men have been blaming their problems on women ever since. Eve blamed the devil. That's another convenient person to put the blame on.

Regardless of their blame transfer, the Bible records that God punished Adam, Eve, and the serpent for their behavior. The moral of the story is simple—regardless of the pressure that people or the devil put on me, it's not an excuse for sin, and I am still responsible before God for my behavior.

I knew a couple years ago who had a very rebellious young son. He was one of the most rebellious, difficult-to-manage children I have ever seen. When he was caught doing something wrong (and it was often), the minute he came under scrutiny of discipline, he would transfer the blame. As soon as the pressure for his behavior began to turn his way, he would begin to cry and say something like, "My friends put a rock in my hand and told me to throw it at that car or they'd make fun of me!"

Instead of seeing through his irresponsibility and blame transfer, his parents would sympathize with him, saying, "Poor Johnny; his friends made him do it." The parents also became immediately adversarial with anyone who called Johnny into account. Even though I'm sure these parents meant well, they were doing a great deal of damage to their son. Rather than teaching him that he was personally responsible for his behavior, they were teaching him that it was all right to transfer the blame and make someone else take the fall.

When my children were growing up, I told them I didn't care how much peer pressure they were under; peer pressure didn't justify misbehavior. Regardless of their excuses, I held them responsible for their actions. Sometimes my kids would come home with lower grades than usual and blame it on their teachers. That didn't work either. I told my children that they had to learn to overcome obstacles and take responsibility for their behavior.

When your kids are fighting among themselves and you break it up, the first thing they do is start blaming each other. We taught our kids to come and get us when someone was doing something he or she shouldn't be doing, and we'd go and take care of it ourselves. We'd gather all the facts, but we'd hold our kids responsible for their behavior in the situation. We didn't care if they whined or moaned or blamed anybody they wanted to; we held them personally responsible for what they did.

The way children learn to take responsibility for their own behavior is, first of all, by watching the examples their parents set for them. If the father blames the mother, the mother blames the father, the parents blame *their* parents, their bosses, the government, or anyone else, their children learn from it. They start to think, "If I can just find someone to blame, I don't have to take responsibility for my behavior."

We need to understand that regardless of what anyone else does, we are personally responsible for our own actions. Jesus hung on the cross, looked down at the people who crucified Him and said, "Father, forgive them." If ever there was a time when a person was justified to seek revenge or do something wrong, it was then. However, Jesus did what was right in spite of the incredible pain, emotional pressure, and persecution He endured.

One day when you are standing before God in judgment, you won't be able to point your finger at others and blame them. On the Day of Judgment, it will be you and God and no one else. If you have lived a life of personal responsibility, not blaming others, the Day of Judgment will be a day of great blessing and reward. However, if you have lived your life blaming others for your failures, mistakes, and sins, the Day of Judgment will be a shocking experience.

In addition to the effect blame transfer has on us and our relationship with God, it also paralyzes us in life. One of the great curses of blaming others is that if other people are the problem, they are also the solution. In other words, because others are the problem, my action won't help; I must wait on them to act. The irresponsible life is a pitiful life, always whining helplessly for parents, government, employers, or someone else to right the wrongs and bring deliverance from the dilemma.

We must teach our children through personal example and training that we are responsible before God for what we do. No one else controls me. I control myself. Because of this, God holds me responsible for how I act. A life encountered with this understanding is much happier and more successful.

SCENE FOUR: The Sin of Cain

God commanded Adam and Eve's sons, Cain and Abel, to bring Him an acceptable offering. In response, Abel brought an offering of his flocks that was acceptable to God. However, Cain brought an offering of his fields that was less than God had required. Therefore, God accepted

Abel's offering and would not accept Cain's. In response to God's preference for Abel's offering, Cain killed him.

"Then the LORD said to Cain, 'Where is Abel your brother?' He said, 'I do not know. Am I my brother's keeper?'" Genesis 4:9

Cain's attitude toward God and his brother Abel was selfish and immature. The essence of his sinful spirit was revealed when he was called into account by God concerning his brother's murder. When God asked him about Abel, Cain arrogantly replied, *"Am I my brother's keeper?"* The answer is yes. God holds us responsible for how we treat our family members and our fellow man.

In a successful family, there is a sense of mutual concern for one another. We look out for each other with an attitude of "if you're not okay, I'm not okay." We protect each other and rally around the person who needs us. That attitude also flows outside of the home to people in our neighborhoods, churches, cities, etc. The attitude that bonds families together and perpetuates a strong society is one of mutual concern for our fellow man.

Jesus had much to say about loving our fellow man. Jesus' personal commandment to His Church was to *"... love one another as I have loved you"* (John 15:12). One day Jesus responded to a question from a man who was trying to justify himself before Jesus. The man had quoted the commandment to Jesus about loving your neighbor as you love yourself. Then the man asked Jesus, "Who is my neighbor?" Jesus' answer was the story of the Good Samaritan (Luke 10:30–36). Jesus expanded the definition of "neighbor" to anyone we encounter in life who is in need and whom we have the resources to help. The entire point of the story of the Good Samaritan was that God holds us responsible to help each other.

In the twenty-fifth chapter of Matthew's Gospel, Jesus reveals an important truth about the end-times judgment of God. God will separate us (referred to as "sheep and goats") from one another in judgment based on the criteria of how we have treated people in this life. Observe the seriousness of Jesus' tone as He speaks about the eternal result of how we have dealt with even the most insignificant levels of society:

*When the Son of Man comes in His glory, and all the holy angels
with Him, then He will sit on the throne of His glory.*
*All the nations will be gathered before Him, and He will separate
them one from another, as a shepherd divides his sheep from
the goats.*
*And He will set the sheep on His right hand, but the goats on
the left.*
*Then the King will say to those on His right hand, "Come, you
blessed of My Father, inherit the kingdom prepared for you from the
foundation of the world: for I was hungry and you gave Me food; I
was thirsty and you gave Me drink; I was a stranger and you took
Me in;*
*"I was naked and you clothed Me; I was sick and you visited Me; I
was in prison and you came to Me."*
*Then the righteous will answer Him, saying, "Lord, when did we
see You hungry and feed You, or thirsty and give You drink?*
*"When did we see You a stranger and take You in, or naked and
clothe You?*
"Or when did we see You sick, or in prison, and come to You?"
*And the King will answer and say to them, "Assuredly, I say
to you,*
*inasmuch as you did it to one of the least of these My brethren, you
did it to Me."*
*Then He will also say to those on the left hand, "Depart from Me,
you cursed, into the everlasting fire prepared for the devil and his
angels: for I was hungry and you gave Me no food; I was thirsty
and you gave Me no drink;*
*"I was a stranger and you did not take Me in, naked and you did
not clothe Me, sick and in prison and you did not visit Me."*
*Then they also will answer Him, saying, "Lord, when did we see
You hungry or thirsty or a stranger or naked or sick or in prison,
and did not minister to You?"*
*Then He will answer them, saying, "Assuredly, I say to you,
inasmuch as you did not do it to one of the least of these, you did not
do it to Me."*

And these will go away into everlasting punishment, but the
righteous into eternal life.
Matthew 25:31–46

God takes the way we treat people personally. People we may judge as being losers, weirdos, or unworthy of our care, He loves. This is something we really need to understand. Not only is selfishness the prevailing spirit of our age, but we are also a very rejecting culture. It's easy to put a judgmental label on someone. However, the same people we reject, God pursues.

As individuals, we need to see people through the eyes of God. Regardless of their faults or social position, God loves people and cares for them. We need to begin in our families by showing concern for each other and by not being selfish or rejecting. A selfless, servant spirit is what Jesus modeled for us. The greatest marriages and families are built with a humble, giving attitude. The worst families are filled with an atmosphere of selfishness, competition, and judgment.

In addition to showing concern for our family members, we also need to be careful about how we talk about and treat people. Children learn to be unmerciful, judgmental, prejudiced, sexist, and bigoted from their parents. They also learn to be compassionate, kind, helpful, and considerate from us. We need to check our attitudes about people and make sure they are consistent with the heart of Jesus. After that, we need to be loving and kind to people of every persuasion. If they are lost, we need to pray for them and witness to them. If they are needy, we need to help them. Regardless of their faults or disposition, we must be careful about how we treat others because we are their keepers. Regardless of whether we acknowledge this responsibility in this life or not, eternity will reveal we are.

SCENE FIVE: The Flood

I'm sure when Adam and Eve were eating of the Tree of the Knowledge of Good and Evil in the garden and were savoring its flavor, they didn't know that their behavior was cursing the generations to come; but it was. We are still paying the penalty for their behavior. Unfortunately, the sinful and selfish heart doesn't really think ahead; it just lives for the moment. The pain of others and the penalty future generations must pay are traded for immediate personal benefit.

Only three chapters after Adam and Eve ate the fruit, the book of Genesis records that God was grieved that He had ever created man. From the seed of sin Adam and Eve had planted in the garden, there was now a harvest of rebellion and corruption to reap. In response to the condition of man at that time, God caused a flood that killed the inhabitants of the earth. Only eight people, Noah and his family, escaped.

We are responsible for how our behavior affects the next generation. Jesus said in Mark 9:42,

> *"But whoever causes one of these little ones who believe in Me to stumble, it would be better for him if a millstone were hung around his neck, and he were thrown into the sea."*

As parents and as members of society, we often underestimate the awesome responsibility we bear for the children around us. This responsibility doesn't just apply to our own children, but it also extends to the children who are affected directly or indirectly by our lives. Both for parents who are laying their children on the altar of their pleasures and for those who are leading this generation astray, there will be a heavy price to pay.

God spoke to Moses in Deuteronomy 5:9 and told him,

> *"... For I, the LORD your God, am a jealous God, visiting the iniquity of the fathers upon the children to the third and fourth generations of those who hate Me."*

God was informing Moses that the sins of disobedient fathers would affect generations after them. As parents, we must understand that our habits, language, attitudes, values, priorities, and lives as a whole are having a direct influence on our great-great-grandchildren. This should raise our level of care about how we live.

Besides God and our mates, children are the most precious things we have in this life. When you touch a child, you are touching the future. If your contact with children is caring and loving, you have blessed the future. If your touch is harmful or negligent, then you have cursed the future.

God holds us responsible to pray for children, to be a good role model to them, to try to reach them for the Lord, and to love them as Christ Himself would. Even though all of us are imperfect and may be overwhelmed with this responsibility, we need to understand that God knows we are weak. He isn't looking for perfection. He is looking for commitment and sincerity. He will forgive our failures when we make mistakes, give us wisdom when we need it, and give us strength for the journey. He is willing and able to give us every resource for success as parents and adults. However, it is our responsibility to take the issue seriously and to properly steward the generation God has put in our care.

SECRET SEVEN

Positive Generational Transference

Good people leave an inheritance to their grandchildren, but the sinner's wealth passes to the godly. Proverbs 13:22 NLT

In successful families, there is a purposeful and positive transference to future generations. Proverbs 13:22 says that "good people," also translated as "the righteous," leave an inheritance to their grandchildren. The virtue being described in this Scripture doesn't just pertain to the distribution of wealth; it is describing the mission and attitude of successful families.

Good parents and grandparents understand the power of their influence over future generations and use it wisely. Because they want to extend the blessings of their lives to their children and future generations, they plan carefully to leave an inheritance for them. This inheritance is more than just money. It consists of righteous values; a good name in the community (Proverbs 22:1); a positive example of marriage, parenting and life skills; demonstrated verbal and physical affection; and spiritual guidance.

The important thing to understand in leaving a good inheritance to future generations is that it never happens by accident. According to Proverbs 13:22, positive generational transference is the result of being a "good" or "righteous" person. In other words, generational transference is the result of our conscious choices regarding values, character, and other important issues.

All of us know that being righteous in this life never happens by accident. We live in a sin-filled world with an evil enemy stalking us daily. Living a life that has a happy ending requires premeditation and some tough choices. If we are willing to live our lives correctly, not only will we be blessed for it, but those blessings will also be passed on to future generations.

Unfortunately, the opposite is also true. When parents sin, unless they repent and change their behavior, their children will always pay a price. This is especially true of parents with children under the age of eighteen who are living in their home. Every action, good or bad, will have a generational impact whether we realize it or not or intend it or not.

Here is a sobering Scripture from the book of Exodus that describes the negative generational effects of the sins of parents upon their children:

> *And the Lord passed before him and proclaimed, "The Lord, the Lord God, merciful and gracious, longsuffering, and abounding in goodness and truth, keeping mercy for thousands, forgiving iniquity and transgression and sin, by no means clearing the guilty, **visiting the iniquity of the fathers upon the children and the children's children to the third and the fourth generation.**"*
> Exodus 34:6–7 (emphasis added)

In this Scripture, God reveals Himself to Moses as the loving, gracious, and forgiving God that He is. However, He also reveals the fact that there will be a generational transference of the negative effects of the sins of the parents upon their children to the third and fourth generation. Here is another way to say it. Everything parents do affects their great-great-grandchildren!

Most parents who live unrighteous lives do so because they don't think about what it will do to their children or future generations. Either that or they are under the delusion that their behavior doesn't really have a great effect upon them.

A perfect example of the wrong mindset that has a negative generational effect upon children is the issue of divorce. Since the mid-20th century, we have been force-fed the lie that divorce is better for parents and children than living in a "bad marriage." "Children are resilient and adaptable," so-called "experts" have said—encouraging adults to conveniently "house hop" and "spouse swap." However, after many years of experiencing the results of divorce, researchers have now proven that the negative effects of divorce not only last a lifetime for children and parents, but they are also generational.[1]

God says in Malachi, chapter 2, that He hates divorce. We must understand that God doesn't hate people who are divorced. He hates the act of divorce because of the lasting damage it inflicts upon the people He loves. Just look around you at the broken families and the heartache of the parents and kids. Some don't have to look beyond their own houses or hearts to see the lasting effects of a wrong decision of the past. Of course, Jesus can heal anyone of anything. A past mistake or problem can always be overcome by faith in Christ. However, we must recognize the long-term devastation of wrong choices if we don't take responsibility for them and turn them to the Lord.

The devil desires to destroy us and to perpetuate that damage to our children and grandchildren. To keep his claim on every generation, he counts on parents to cooperate with him—because when they do, it makes it much easier for him to destroy their children and to continue the cycle of generational failure. As parents, we must realize the spiritual and practical effects of our behavior, good and bad, and decide to make whatever choices and changes are necessary to make a positive generational transference to our children and future generations.

The mindset the devil loves is a self-centered, "now" oriented perspective. If he can just get parents, grandparents, and authority figures to think about themselves and what they want today, rather than thinking about their children and the future, he can get them to rationalize almost any kind of behavior. This is exactly what is happening in our nation.

Recently, I saw a father walking into a store with two elementary-aged girls I assumed were his daughters. Not only was this man very rough looking, but he was also wearing a tee shirt with horrible vulgarity on it like I had never seen in public. I remember looking at that man and wondering to myself what he was thinking when he justified putting that shirt on and wearing it in front of those two impressionable young girls. That isn't even counting all of the other children who saw his shirt that day and all of the other days he wore it. Needless to say, his behavior was selfish and short-sighted.

As I stated earlier, a positive generational transference always occurs on purpose. It happens because a "good" person considers his children's destiny and begins investing in them and in their future. Successful families are the result of this type of behavior. The more generations that make a positive transference to their children, the more of a legacy and a good inheritance are transferred.

Maybe you are the product of a righteous legacy today and you know what a blessing it is. Or maybe you have come from a bad past and a tragic family history and you want to be the person who breaks the sinful generational cycle and begins a legacy for the future. Here is some valuable information to help all of us to understand the specifics of how to leave a righteous inheritance for future generations.

Recently, I read a fascinating book by a lawyer named James Hughes, Jr. The book is titled, *Family Wealth: Keeping It in the Family*.2 In his book, James Hughes, Jr. shares his insights as to how a family can perpetuate wealth for generations. He travels extensively around the world, teaching wealthy people how to keep their money in the family as a positive generational transference.

As all of us know, many families leave an inheritance to their children only for it to be squandered. "Shirt sleeves to shirt sleeves in three generations" is the old adage that describes the futility many have experienced in trying to perpetuate wealth. In fact, so many people believe that leaving money to their children will ruin them, a surprising number of wealthy people give most or all of their money to charities, foundations, and religious groups upon their death, leaving little or nothing to their children.

Two very well-known individuals who fall into this category are Bill Gates and Warren Buffett. Both billionaires, they have publicly stated that they will leave very little of their massive fortunes to their children because of their belief that it will ruin them and they will surely lose it.

This is the unfortunate thinking that James Hughes, Jr. encounters in wealthy families that keeps them from being able to transfer wealth from generation to generation. However, according to him, many families transfer wealth from generation to generation very successfully. His book describes the principles of successful wealth transference from his experience with many families who have done it.

The point I'm trying to make about all of this isn't how to transfer money (even though it is included). It is that we must reject any thought system that excuses us from transferring what God has given us to our children and grandchildren in a responsible manner. Not only can we succeed, but we must succeed. Our children's future and the future of our families are depending on it.

To do this, we must reject the defeatist and irresponsible thinking that leads to failure. On one extreme are those who think little of the effects of their behavior and how their children will suffer in the future for their foolishness and lack of consideration. On the other extreme are those who do consider their children, but throw up their hands in defeat because they believe it is futile to try to transfer wealth or any other blessing from generation to generation. This is the "every generation is on its own" mentality, and it is wrong.

Many parents believe that their job is just to feed and clothe their kids, give them a decent education, and then "they're on their own." However, the Bible says that the effects of successful parenting are generational. In successful families, parents have a mission and attitude of total transference of every blessing of life to their children and grandchildren.

This is why Proverbs 13:22 says that a "good" person leaves an inheritance to his children's children. Good and righteous people plan their lives so that they are still blessing their families long after they are gone. This is a stark contrast to the thinking of the irresponsible parents who either don't care about their children's future enough to order their lives accordingly or those who believe it doesn't matter.

Not only does the Bible say that we can transfer good things to future generations, but it also tells us we must. In fact, as I have stated earlier, there is no such thing as a parent who doesn't make a generational transference to his children and grandchildren. The only issue is—will it be positive or negative?

In his book concerning the generational transference of wealth, James Hughes, Jr., makes some interesting points about families who transfer wealth successfully. Even though his book is secular, I believe all of these points are highly Biblical, and they explain why those who practice these principles succeed.

I will summarize three principles for perpetuating wealth that I have gleaned from James Hughes' book and the Biblical principles that coincide with them. I believe these principles will help you understand how to transfer good things to your children and grandchildren and how to teach them to do the same. The three principles for positive transference to future generations are:

1. There must be a value system with love as the highest virtue.

James Hughes, Jr. observes that families who perpetuate wealth for many generations are always those who love each other deeply and communicate that love as their greatest virtue. In fact, families who perpetuate wealth successfully categorize wealth in three ways and in this order:

1. Human wealth—The intrinsic value of every member of the family individually

2. Intellectual wealth—The deposit of knowledge, learning, and education that is invested in family members
3. Financial wealth—The financial wealth of the family that exists for the purpose of serving the family

In successful families, money isn't the most important thing; people are. If parents communicate to their children that they are servants of money, a family business, a sports legacy, a religious institution, or anything that subverts their value to that of something else, children will not buy into it or perpetuate it.

The only thing that is commonly held as a high value to all— every generation, every race, every political persuasion, both God and man, male and female, young and old—is love. To uphold love as the highest value of the family is to ensure success. To choose any other value system is to ensure failure. That is why Jesus told us as His Church that we must love one another.

"This is My commandment, that you love one another as I have loved you"
John 15:12

Jesus knew that the work of the Church could not be perpetuated unless the highest virtue was love. Today, many churches and religious institutions that espouse high standards of "truth" or boast of glories past are empty edifices that testify to this truth. Because some value other than love became the standard of their existence, they stopped meeting needs, being gracious, and attracting those outside to come in and those inside to keep coming back. The followers became the servants of a "truth," cause, or tradition. As good as they may be, they are not good enough.

Love is the only virtue that can guarantee success and positive generational transference. By the way, the definition of "love" is the model of Christ. True love is a selfless, servant-hearted behavior that does the right thing regardless of feelings or circumstances. When properly practiced, it is the most powerful force on earth.

2. There must be a vision for the future that includes the next generation.

In his book, James Hughes, Jr. reveals that families who successfully perpetuate wealth have a family mission statement along with a financial plan that looks ahead up to one hundred years. Anything less than fifty year planning is considered short-term.

In the Bible, there are two powerful verses that talk about the importance of vision for the future. The first is Proverbs 29:18a. It says,

"Where there is no vision, the people perish" (KJV)

This literally means that when people don't have a sense of spiritual insight or revelation concerning their lives today and their futures tomorrow, it isn't possible to restrain negative behavior or to keep a group together on the same mission.

The old saying goes, "If you fail to plan, you plan to fail." The reason many people don't succeed at imparting a positive generational transference to their children and grandchildren is because they have no plan or vision. As I stated earlier, positive generational transference never happens by accident. It happens because a good person makes up his mind that he is going to do it.

Do you have a vision for your family? If not, you need to ask God for one. Regardless of whether you are single or married, with or without children, you should hit your knees in prayer and ask God what His plan is for your life, marriage, and family. Then, you should seek God until He answers you specifically and you get a "vision" or an inner sense of what He is saying. Once you receive what you believe is God's will for your life and future, write it down and keep it before you. Make it the mission statement of your life.

Look at this powerful Scripture from Habakkuk 2:2:

"... Write the vision and make it plain on tablets, that he may run who reads it."

An extraordinary truth found in this Scripture is the fact that writing a vision down and reading it regularly energizes our lives and our children as we train them according to it. As Habakkuk says, the one who reads it "may run." Vision is a motivating and powerful force. The opposite is also true.

Without a vision for our lives, marriages, families, finances, ministries, and the important things in life, we don't know where we are going. Every day is filled with "going through the motions" with no greater meaning. Also, when we have no vision, our lives naturally degrade.

Because we have no clear vision, our behavior is both unrestrained and unmotivated. Living this way for a long period of time results in a meaningless life and the failure to transfer anything positive to our children.

It is critical that we have a plan for our future and know what we are trying to accomplish. Here are some important questions to ask yourself and answer in learning to have a positive generational effect upon your family:

- What is God's call for your life?
- What do you want your children to remember about you after you're gone?
- What do you want said about you at your funeral?
- What is the purpose of your marriage?
- If you died today, what would be your greatest regret?
- What do you want your children to become, and what are you doing to help them accomplish it?
- Do you have a clear plan for your life that you have written down and look at regularly to keep you on track and to measure your progress?
- What do you need to be doing that you are not doing to leave a positive generational transference?

When you sit down and begin considering some of these questions, it helps to lift your eyes above the fray of everyday life to see the big picture. Seeing the big picture, keeping that picture before you, and making sure it's the picture God wants for you are major factors in deciding your future and that of your children and grandchildren.

3. Every generation must be discipled as responsible stewards of what they have received.

In his book, James Hughes, Jr. reveals why certain families succeed in perpetuating wealth where others fail. Families who succeed in perpetuating wealth train up their children as "first generation" wealth producers who build and steward their wealth to serve the family and future generations.

The reason many families witness the financial failure and personal destruction caused by inherited wealth left to their children is because they don't take the time and energy to disciple them in how to use it and the greater meaning of it. Simply leaving a financial inheritance for your children means little if character, knowledge, and purpose don't accompany it.

Regardless of how much money they have or don't have, parents are responsible for discipling and mentoring their children. The Bible specifically charges parents, especially fathers, with the responsibility of diligently training their children (Ephesians 6:4/Deuteronomy 6:6–9). Many parents reject this responsibility outright. Others transfer the responsibility to schools, churches, or technology as their replacements as they take little time or energy to train their children.

It's never too late to do the right thing. Begin today to think about your future and the future of your family.

Proverbs 22:6 instructs parents,

> *"Train up a child in the way he should go, and when he is old he will not depart from it."*

This promise is powerful, but it is many times ignored or

misunderstood. It tells us that if we "train up" our children in the correct way, when they are old (mature), they won't depart from the way we have trained them.

To claim this promise, we must meet the condition of training up our children. In order for us to do this, we must understand that training isn't just saying something to our children or telling them the correct thing to do. Training means that we show them, assist them, mentor them, disciple them, and teach them.

Training is the full process of transferring values, character, knowledge, spirituality, skills, and purpose to our children. It includes everything we do and excludes nothing. Wise parents understand the power of their example and use it to their advantage. They take time and effort to transfer the values, knowledge, and skills to their children that they will need to succeed in their future. This takes quality and quantity time because there is no such thing as successful part-time parenting.

Also, because love is the exalted virtue, the children feel valued and accept what is being transferred to them. They are willing to uphold their parents' instruction later in life as they transfer it to their own children. Children who are well-trained and greatly loved are those who are most likely to "buy in" to the generational mindset that perpetuates a healthy and successful family.

Sadly, people who fail to make a positive generational transference to their children don't take the time and effort to teach and train them. Can anyone wonder why these children fail later in life? It is frustrating to hear a person of wealth state that he won't leave his fortune to his children because it will ruin them or "they can't handle it." If that same parent had faith in his children and took the time to train them properly, things would be different. This is what the Bible says, and it is the experience of James Hughes, Jr. with families who successfully perpetuate wealth.

Successful families are successful for a reason. They make right choices and think the way the Bible tells us we should think. One other thing about successful families—anyone can have one! Regardless of the mistakes, pain, or failures of your past, God can forgive you, heal you, and give you the power to succeed. It's never too late to do the right thing. Begin today to think about your future and the future of your family. Be diligent in planning and working to make a positive generational transference.

---

1 Wallerstein, Judith S., *The Unexpected Legacy of Divorce: A 25 Year Landmark Study*, ed. Judith Wallerstein, Julia M. Lewis and Sandra Blakeslee (New York: Hyperion. 200).

2 Hughes, Jr., James E., *Family Wealth: Keeping It In The Family* (Princeton Junction, NJ: Net Wrx, Inc., 1997).

ABOUT THE AUTHOR

Jimmy Evans is Senior Pastor of Gateway Church, a multi-campus church in the Dallas/Fort Worth Metroplex. Since it began in 2000, the church has grown to more than 36,000 active members.

Jimmy is the Founder and CEO of MarriageToday, a ministry that is devoted to helping couples thrive in strong and fulfilling marriages and families. Jimmy and his wife Karen co-host MarriageToday, a nationally syndicated television program. He also serves as the Senior Elder of Trinity Fellowship Church in Amarillo, Texas. Jimmy holds an Honorary Doctorate of Literature from The Kings University and has authored more than seventeen books.

Jimmy and Karen have been married for 45 years and have two married children and five grandchildren.

ALSO BY JIMMY EVANS

Marriage on the Rock

Marriage On The Rock: Couple's Discussion Guide (Workbook)

Blending Families

Blending Families Workbook and DVD Series (Workbook)

7 Secrets of Successful Families

Freedom From Your Past: A Christian Guide to Personal Healing and Restoration

The Stress-Free Marriage

One Devotional : 52 Weekly Marriage-Building Devotions for Thriving Couples

The Keys to Sexual Fulfillment in Marriage: Creating an Atmosphere of Sexual Pleasure in Your Marriage

Happy, Happy Love

A Mind Set Free

Mountaintop of Marriage: A Vision Retreat Guidebook (Workbook)

The Overcoming Life

Our Secret Paradise

Return to Intimacy

By: Karen Evans

From Pain to Paradise

Made in the USA
Monee, IL
12 January 2021